D0174529

LEARNING TO LEARN:
MAXIMIZING YOUR PERFORMANCE POTENTIAL

D. Trinidad Hunt

Élan Enterprises
47-430 Hui Nene St.
Kaneohe, Hawaii 96744
(800) 707-ELAN, Fax (808) 239-2482
Email: elantrin@aol.com

DEDICATION

I dedicate this work to both my grandparents for it is their sweet spirit that dances through the pages and lingers in the language of the heart. In all my works, may I do justice to the sacred trust they bequeathed to others through me.

ACKNOWLEDGMENTS

Learning to Learn was born out of the love and support of many. The writing and development of this piece was a joyful event because of them. May Spirit return to each one of them a hundred-fold what they have given to me.

• To our great mother, the Pacific Ocean, whose vast wisdom whispered in the wind as I gazed incessantly into her translucent turquoise waves. You have been there for me since my birth in the islands and played a special part in the writing of this book.

• To Leighton Mau, whose suggestion initiated the writing of this book. Were it not for your constant support, I may never have begun this work.

• To Craig Neddersen and the management and staff of the Kona Surf Resort for all that they gave during the first three drafts of this text. It was your very special Aloha that lifted me when I was down and nurtured me when I was up.

• To Renee Gomes, Diane Takushi, Sheryl Sakuma, Russell Mau, Lester Higa, and Greg Valen of Hawaii Business Equipment, Inc. for being who they are. None of this work would have been possible without your ever present spirit and consistent actions. In all that I do, you are there.

• To Rolinda Harris for just being. Your heart is ever full of love; thank-you dear friend.

• To my parents, for you are always with me.

• To Michelle M. Jerin whose editing support consistently enhanced this book. The wonderful energy and vitality that you bring has added a special joy to all that we do together.

• And finally, it is with special honor that I acknowledge my business associate, Lynne Truair. Your love has enfolded and protected these pages. Thank-you for your friendship; it has always provided a safe haven for the development and nurturing of all aspects of this work.

TABLE OF CONTENTS

Section Two
Power Skills for the 21st Century

Section Three
Behavioral Change Skills

INTRODUCTION

The word education comes from the Latin root "educere" which means "to draw out." It will take the drawing out of our latent and full potential to answer both the demands and challenges that our future holds. As Michelangelo delivered "David" from the stone, so mankind shall be delivered from the narrow ties and restrictions of his past, set free to actualize his latent and full performance potential. Thus, as the wave of change breaks on a new shore, we sense the arrival of a timeless new era in which our lives will be a demonstration of learning, growth and development.

We must maximize our performance potential for therein lies the obvious next step in the shifting paradigm of personal and professional effectiveness. *Learning to Learn* addresses the quality of life that is available when we stretch to attain this potential through a lifelong commitment to learning. A fully actualized human being is born of the marriage of both character development and skills. Consequently, *Learning to Learn* includes both the cultivation of character as well as the development of learning skills appropriate to our true humanity and the landscape of the future, the landscape of the 21st century.

A PERSONAL NOTE FROM THE AUTHOR

"Each of us is a cell in a greater body: the
body of humankind. To be a human
being is to be a human being regardless
of race, color, creed or country. And,
once we truly understand ourselves, we
in fact understand each other."

D. Trinidad Hunt

*Grow yourself and growth will happen around you, for life
is really about learning and growth, and learning and
growth are why we are here.*

During the course of my last 25 years in the field of
education, I have discovered much of what I am sharing in
the following pages. I began my exploration of learning in
the classroom, and finally, finding the system too confin-
ing, left the traditional fields of education bound on a
journey of discovery in the realm of human potential.

My journey took me far from the hallowed halls of
learning into the streets and byways of business. I formed
a company in 1978 that focused on organizational training.
We worked with chief executive officers and front-line
people and at the same time instituted training programs for
all branches and ranks of the military.

Still not satisfied with what I had learned about learning
and behavioral change, I began searching for a community
project that I could "sink my teeth" into. I discovered that
there was a need for education within the prison systems.
The result of this discovery was the inception of a three-hour
weekly program at the Women's Community Correction
Center on Oahu. During the course of this two-year period
results of our work proved very exciting as more than 70
inmates successfully completed prison terms and re-emerged
as contributing members in the community.

Several years later I formed a new business alliance and continued along the same lines of educational exploration. At that time we began offering long-term organizational trainings focusing on the shift from the old business model of management, management from the top down, to the new model of management by involvement and empowerment. At the same time, I renewed my interest in community work and my partner and I began offering trainings and assemblies for thousands of students within the school systems. The results were immediate and gratifying. The student body leaders in one school were so encouraged about what they had learned in a single session on leadership that they pooled their funds to bring us in to train their teachers.

Today, our time is focused in three major areas. Élan Enterprises' work is divided between organizational training; educating people in leading edge business and learning skills, and The Academy Élan; a training program designed for those seeking a successful and fulfilling life. Our remaining time is dedicated to World Youth Network International, a non-profit organization that is committed to preparing today's students with the skills equal to the challenges that humanity will face in the new millennium.

Anyone with a normal, healthy body and brain can expand both the quality and quantity of their learning as well as accelerate their learning time. *Learning to Learn* is a result of thousands of hours of teaching with thousands of individuals in hundreds of training rooms across the nation. As a trainer and educator I know that the simple principles and techniques presented here do work, for they come to you already pretested. We have worked with every concept, from the opening paradigm shift, to the creative principles, to the behavioral change skills. Thousands of individuals have used these principles to enrich their lives and so can you.

Learning to Learn may be the most important developmental commitment a person of the 21st century could make!

P.S.

This manuscript is coming to you from Hawaii, not because I wanted it to, but because life itself dictated that it should. I was born and raised in the Hawaiian Islands, and although I received my higher education and worked for 13 years on the mainland, one day Hawaii reclaimed her child and called me home. At this very moment, I am sitting at my computer overlooking the legendary outline of the Kona Coast; a shoreline of black lava carved jagged in an emerald green-blue sea, splashed by brilliant white breakers of crystal ocean foam.

Although I continue to travel to the mainland for my work, the islands always insist upon my return. Hawaii whispers a secret language all its own. The heart of Hawaii is deep, the way of Hawaii is healing, and the pulse of Hawaii is love. Is it not natural that life would want this text to be delivered from the sacred shores of these ancient isles? Possibly there is something in the ways of the ancients that needs to re-emerge in this new era, something deep and everlasting for a new generation facing the challenges of a new period in the history of mankind.

Maybe the message that longs to be delivered lies in the motto of old Hawaii, for it speaks of education in the truest sense of the word: "The life of the land is preserved in righteousness." Here an educated man was a wise man, not in the ways of knowledge but in the ways of universal principles. Mankind is facing a transformation and the voices of our past are asking to be integrated with our own. It is our hope, both mine and the voice of the ancients who whisper through me, that this book touches and awakens not only the intellect but also the heart of each of you who encounter it.

It is not by accident that this small volume has found its way into your hands. It has come to you because of an inner ripening; your readiness has called it to you. Thus, each of you who read it will find that it speaks to you in a very special way. If you allow this little book to do its work, it will help you turn your learning and growth, the very process of your life experience, into a meaningful and delightful journey fueled by the adventure of learning. Remember, that as human beings, part of our purpose is to contribute to life in some small way. As our love of learning and our spontaneous ability to learn is restored, our contribution expands effortlessly. As we change ourselves the personal world around us changes, impacting our family, our profession and the community at large.

As we approach the horizon of the 21st century, may wisdom be the guiding star that helps each of us as we shape a new context for life and learning!

D.Trinidad Hunt
Hawaii

SECTION ONE

CREATING THE CONTEXT FOR LEARNING TO LEARN

Chapter One

WE ARE ALL NATURAL LEARNERS

*"Knowledge is a function of intellect
while wisdom is a function of being."*

D. Trinidad Hunt

Good morning! This is your wake-up call to transformation! For the first time in written history we are standing at the threshold of opportunity viewing a new horizon of stunning potential and breathtaking possibility.

Behind us, the limited scope of the past, before us the unexplored possibility available in human experience. The horizon is as compelling as it is provocative in nature, for it holds an opportunity never before available in human experience, an opportunity to make a quantum leap into a totally new way of being. We are standing in the face of a very real question, "What does it mean to be a human being?" not as an extrapolation from the past, but as a creative possibility for the future.

We are living in one of the most exciting and critical periods in the recorded history of our planet. With the

Industrial Age behind us and the Information Age well underway, we have found that our focus has shifted from moving mass to moving information. Where once the U.S. Steel Corporation was the giant of the Western world, today the microchip industry - the mass market for information management - has fast become the focus of a new generation.

Course curriculums in universities across the nation and the world reflect this new interest in information exchange. Entire departments have been established to study communication at the personal, business, and community levels, as well as at the national and international levels. Simultaneously, the old-world order based on personal agendas and control is collapsing on every front. Families are going through renewal, organizations are restructuring, nations are declaring their freedom and countries that were once diametrically opposed are now communicating with one another. Throughout the world people and relationships are emerging in a new way. The wave of transformation has begun.

At the same time, the ecological challenges facing both ourselves and the upcoming generations are escalating, pressing us to fully embrace our role and responsibility in the health and well-being of our planet. We are at a turning point, a critical juncture in our history. Mankind is being called upon to make a quantum leap, for we cannot continue to create our future out of our past. Yet, this calling of mankind is a calling of a very personal nature; not one of us is exempt from the responsibility of our own humanity. We are faced with embracing a new world order where each of us, no matter what the country or the creed, shall come to take full responsibility for ourselves and each other.

What worked for us in the old order will not work for us now and although this is no small confrontation, as human beings we are capable of rising to the occasion of the challenges at hand. There is a world to be restored, both figuratively and literally, and each of us is being called upon to bear the responsibility of restoration in our personal lives. What requires healing in ourselves will be reflected in our intimate and job-related relationships. We are each being called upon to bring harmony and renewal to everything that isn't working in our lives. In the final analysis, our healing shall be experienced and expressed through the re-emergence of trust and a renewal of relationship at all levels.

As we close the doors on the 20th century and turn our sights to the year 2100, we find that the precipice upon which we are standing overlooks a territory of vast new and exciting dimensions. The landscape of the future will be both process- and product-oriented. And the character of the future will be the unfettered personality, an individual of limitless dimensions: educated, compassionate, coura-geous, a visionary willing to take a stand for the birth of a new world.

Vision is critical here, for it is the bridge between this world and the world of possibility. It is the chrysalis holding the hope of flight or the genius in ourselves that is waiting to be realized. It's the tale that's never been told, and the song that has never been sung. Vision is what makes life worth living; for visionaries see a desired future state, and this transforms a menial task into magic. Vision's locus of power is internal for it lights a fire deep within the heart. To live a life of purpose, meaning and lasting joy, further, to transform ourselves and ultimately our planet, we must allow ourselves to be the natural visionaries that we are. Vision is the link between the infinite and the finite. We must consciously hold within our hearts a deep sense of the sacred bond that links us to our work and our connection with all life. It is this conscious awareness that makes the difference between mediocrity and genius in any given field of endeavor.

On this path of transformation, vision gives birth to our mission; for a mission takes the vision out of the thinking or dreaming stage into the action or activity stage. Whether a vision be personal, organizational, national, or planetary in scope, it has the power to uplift and protect us from the bumps and "stuff" of daily living. It is a tremendous motivator, having the capacity and power to bring an individual or group of people to a place they've never been. It makes tasks bearable, persistence easier, and gives a sense of exhilaration to the work at hand.

Humanity has begun to come home to itself; we have discovered that we were our own worst enemy, and now we must become our own best friend on our life's journey. At the heart of this new model of transformation, is possibility in its most awesome context; that which lies in its latent potentialized state. Like Adam, awaiting the touch of the master's hand in Michelangelo's creation, this domain of possibility is being born out of the firmament.

The alchemical combination for this full potentializing of the human being, seems to lie in the process of discovering our purpose and then realizing our purpose and vision together, as the family of man who is responsible for this planet. There is a high premium placed on adaptability, for there is no permanency in the new model, only an unswerving belief in the human being and the human ability to create, adapt, innovate, grow and change. In this process-oriented model, people and organizations are becoming the new domain of possibility for human development, creativity, and the exploration of human interdependence. The transformation is exhilarating, if not somewhat heady, in that all of the features of the old paradigm have been totally dislocated in time and space. Transformation is seen as an ongoing, endless, dynamic process which is never complete! The path of transformation then, must begin with the question:

WHAT DOES IT MEAN TO BE A HUMAN BEING?

Photography has awakened us to the possibility of changing our lens of life to gain a more powerful perspective of a subject. For example, you can zoom in to catch the heart of a flower or zoom back to view the entire branch upon which the flower rests. Using this photographic model for a moment, let us change the lens of our viewing to gain a clearer vision of the landscape of learning.

The lens we are going to use is a twofold question, *"What does it mean to be a human being, and why are we here anyway?"* As we view life through this lens we find that our perception of learning begins to shift from something we have to do in order to keep up with the pace of the future to something that we were born to do. Let us use a metaphor to gain the full contextual shift available from approaching life and learning from the vantage point provided by this question. As you continue reading, use your mind as well as every aspect of your being. Listen from your own still center as the metaphor unfolds and something deep within responds to its tone.

Consider this:

If you and I were going on a trip to the moon, we would leave Earth and travel through space on a spaceship until we arrived in the moon's atmosphere. Once there, we might decide that we wanted to explore the moon's surface. What would we need wear in order to leave the space craft and survive while walking on the moon for a few days?

In order to sustain life on the moon for even a brief amount of time, we would obviously need to live in space suits. These suits would have to be created specifically to assist us in maintaining and supporting life in the moon's atmosphere. They would be pressurized and connected to an oxygen supply and they would need to be flexible enough to allow the mobility necessary to move freely in space. In other words, the suits would have to be designed to serve the purpose and needs of the specific journey we were embarking upon.

Furthermore, if the National Aeronautics and Space Administration was preparing us for the trip, this space research agency's ground team would provide us with a thorough training in the use of the suit. We might also assume that the NASA team would provide us with a training manual for future reference.

●●●

When we come to live on Earth it is very much like going to live on the moon in that we have to take a space suit in order to survive. Our space suit on this planet is called a body and it was designed specifically for life on Earth. No one can check in on the planet without taking one and no one can live here without wearing one.

Now, the only difference between getting a space suit to go to the moon and getting our body suit to live here is that we didn't receive instructions or a manual with our body. It might have been a lot easier if there had been a Planetary Welcoming Committee when we arrived. We might have spent some time with them in the hospital nursery receiving a basic training on *The Body - It's Purpose and Use While You Are Here on Earth.*

Had we had that training, it probably would have gone something like this:

"Welcome to Planet Earth. You have just received a basic baby body suit which will be on loan to you for the duration of your visit here. During your stay you will be responsible for its proper care and feeding. You will be expected to grow it, mature it and age it. For the next 80-100 years Earth will be your home, a place for learning and growth in the human experience. Your body suit was designed specifically to assist you in learning so that you can accomplish your life goals while you are here on Earth. At the end of your visit you will be expected to return your body suit, for neither it, nor anything else that you acquire during your stay, can be taken with you upon departure. At that time you will leave with nothing more than a record. This record will include a history of all your life events as well as your learning experiences and development as a compassionate loving human being."

In other words, what we would discover in our nursery training room is that the very nature of life on Earth is learning. *In fact, planet Earth is a giant classroom and each of us living here is a student.* As students we are here to learn, for on Earth learning and growth are integral components of the transformation process that will continue as long as we're living on the planet. Like our space suits which were designed to sustain life on the moon, our body suits have been perfectly constructed to sustain life on Earth for an extended period of time. The only difference between the two suits is functional. Our space suits were created to support life for a brief exploration on the moon while our body suits were designed to suit Earth's purpose of learning and growth. In other words, our body suits were created specifically to assist us in the learning necessary to develop and refine our character, reach our performance potential, and accomplish our lifetime goals in service to mankind.

THE HUMAN BODY IS A NATURAL LEARNING SUIT

Thus, we come to discover that part of what it means to be a human being is to be born into a body that was built to learn. Without any formal education, a child between the ages of birth and seven absorbs an entire cultural heritage and at least one language, if not two or three in the case of bi- or multilingual homes. For, it is the function of the mind to merge with what it focuses on. If that child happens to be a boy, by the age of seven he has learned to swagger like daddy and has developed some of the dominant personality traits of his closest male models. For the young female, primping in front of the mirror, trying on high heels and testing mother's lipstick, usually begins by age seven.

As adults we completely assume that this natural learning process will occur so that we only become aware of it when it *doesn't* happen. For example, if the child doesn't begin to respond to language or imitate members of the family in the first few years of life, apprehension sets in regarding the child's development. In fact, a parent who notices that the learning process is not occurring naturally, will usually take the child to a family doctor for a thorough checkup, concerned that the body suit might be malfunctioning.

There is an old Catholic axiom that states "give me a child between the ages of birth and seven and I'll give you a Catholic forever." The body was constructed to learn by a process much like osmosis in which the child, like a sponge, absorbs everything from the culture and environment into which he or she was born.

Because of this remarkable way in which the brain and body work, everything in a child's environment forms a blueprint of possibility for that child's development. The models that surround a child determine the quality and character of that child's experience and ultimately of that child's expression. *The child will imprint the behaviors of the adults in his environment whether or not those behaviors are healthy*, for whatever the child loves, he will become.

THE PERFECT COMPUTER AND RECORDING STUDIO

Add to this the miraculous power of the brain to record its every experience, and we can begin to understand the explicit ease with which learning to learn can occur. The human brain is one of the most powerful centralized memory systems ever created. Not only does it interact with its environment but it also records every interaction as it is occurring.

It is as if each of us has our own perfect video recording studio inside our heads. The brain records every event in our lives down to the minute details. If we were to go back to our fourth birthday under hypnosis, we would be able to replay the event in its entirety. We would see the children who were there, the cake and candles, and we would hear the birthday song as it was being sung at that time.

If that is not enough, the brain never ceases in its centralized function. It continues recording and working day and night regardless of whether we are awake or asleep. It records our dreams and engages in solutions to our daily problems. It delivers messages and analyzes events in our lives, developing the best possible behavioral choices for both personal and professional relationship experiences.

Every good computer comes with an operator's manual however, we did not receive a manual with our bodies so operating them for optimal learning has remained a mystery. You will discover that the following chapters provide a manual for utilizing your body and mind in order to maximize your performance potential.

At times during the course of the text we shall refer to the body and mind as a single learning system called the body suit. You will discover the power of the body suit (mind and body) to interact with its environment, absorb it, problemsolve, and record the entire process while it is occurring, and this will indeed become our gateway to freedom on our path of transformation. We will discover that our performance potential is infinite and we will learn to think with our whole body utilizing the totality of the system's ability to learn.

Use your life as your own personal learning laboratory by applying what you discover in the reading of this book. As the chapters progress, and you test, try, and apply the material, you will begin to recover your natural ability to learn as well as your spontaneous love for discovery and growth.

Remember to remember who you are and why you are here!

POWER POINTS

❀

Planet Earth is a giant classroom and the very
nature of life on Earth is learning.

❀

The human body is a natural learning suit
designed specifically to assist us in our
development while we are on Earth.

❀

The brain, as the central unit of the body suit,
works day and night to support us in our life work.

❀

Children learn by osmosis; what they love,
they eventually become.

❀

Remember to remember who you are
and why you are here.

Chapter Two

BLOCKS, BARRIERS
AND BREAKTHROUGHS

"What usually happens in the educational process is that the faculties are dulled, overloaded, stuffed, and paralyzed so that by the time most people are mature they have lost their innate capabilities."

Buckminster Fuller

In order to make a quantum leap in learning, we must first understand the internal processes that influence our ability to learn. In other words, if we are all natural learners and our bodies were designed to support that function, then what blocks us from learning? What slows the learning process? Why does it seem at times that learning requires so much work?

BLOCKS TO LEARNING

Stop and consider your own experience of learning for a

moment and ask yourself, "What is it that slows my learning? When is learning a struggle for me? When do I find my learning blocked and exactly what blocks it?"

As we explore the questions of our blocks to learning you will notice that many of the ties that have bound us have been unconscious beliefs and attitudes from the past. From the moment of birth we have received messages from those around us about our capabilities, our actions and our performance. Parental models have left their imprint and peer pressure as well as pressure from our teachers has influenced our behavior and shaped our personalities. Conscious and unconscious programming has often been counterproductive, creating limited perceptions of ourselves and our abilities. These limited perceptions have left us somewhat dysfunctional, if not totally crippled, in our operative learning proficiencies.

The Belief Barrier

Can you remember the ecstasy during the early years of learning? Probably very little or not at all because those early experiences have so often been overlaid with years of reactive situations in which unconscious interactions diminished our personal esteem and confidence.

In kindergarten the teacher's questions elicited an excited response from almost everyone. Learning was an exhilarating passion for most of us then but when teacher told Johnny his answer was wrong, we all got the message. By second grade there were fewer active responses and by fifth grade only a few extremely brave or very smart students dared to throw their hands into the air. It doesn't take much to damage a child's tender esteem or destroy a child's interest and by ninth grade most of us didn't care anymore. We were into puberty and had switched our attention to members of the opposite sex; it wasn't "in" to be actively interested in learning.

By graduation and college learning had been turned into a cat-and-mouse game. "Acing it" was getting the best grades possible with the least amount of work: Being in and accepted was being able to cut classes and still cruise by. Is it any wonder that upon being catapulted into The Information Age and told that learning to learn is fast becoming the number one skill of the 21st century we are afraid we can't make the grade?

Our beliefs about ourselves keep us grounded: inhibited personal esteem, lowered self-confidence, an instinctive feeling that I'm a con-artist who just scraped by. All of these unconscious imprints from our childhood have created hidden fears and fleeting images of inadequacy. We don't usually admit these feelings publicly, but often, just beneath the surface of our awareness, lie slight but haunting self-doubts that damper our ability as natural learners.

BELIEFS SHAPE OUR EXPERIENCES

Beyond the window of our beliefs lies the world of our experience, for our beliefs shape and color our experience. If the window we view life through is a window of limitations our behavior will exhibit limitations. If the window is a belief in the unlimited capabilities of the mind and body and our ability as human beings to bring about a change in our lives, we open ourselves to the vast performance potential that is available to all of us.

Our most critical beliefs are the beliefs we hold about our capabilities. Thus, in order to make a quantum leap in learning, we must make way for a new set of positive beliefs by releasing the disabling beliefs of our past. This is easily accomplished by reframing our experience. Just as changing the frame on a picture changes what is highlighted within the scene, so reframing our experience changes the highlights of that experience. As we reframe the landscape of our beliefs about ourselves in relationship to learning we will experience a shift from disablement to empowerment, from limitation to infinite possibility.

Notice what happens to your view of learning as you internalize the following two statements:

> "The truth is that we are probably geniuses; we barely use 5 percent of our ability, and yet we've done extremely well so far in life."
>
> *Lead the Field*

> "If we could get our brains to function at half of their inherent capacity, we could learn forty languages, memorize an encyclopedia from cover to cover, and complete the required courses of three dozen colleges."
>
> *Lead the Field*

By reframing our experience we open the way to wonder, and wonder is the fuel for our learning journey. "I wonder what would be possible if....

...I *really could* learn another language?

...I *could* tap another 5 percent of my potential?
...I really was without any learning limitations?

The Barriers of Fear

Fear #1: Fear of Failure
Known as "the paralyzing fear," fear of failure has a crippling effect: It often immobilizes us even before we begin. Those who are caught by the fear of failure are often paralyzed at the onset of a project. In this case one's personal identity and sense of self-worth has become associated with succeeding; failure means to have failed as a person.

Fear always causes us to contract while life is just the opposite; life is expansive and energizing. Hence, the antidote for this fear is a philosophical reframe plus an action step. The reframe is this: *Life works, get out of the way and let it!* The action step is to begin a small activity and take it all the way through to completion.

As you engage in the activities that move you toward your goal, pay close attention to what works and doesn't work. Study every setback, viewing it as an opportunity for learning. As we set small goals and achieve small goals our self-confidence goes up, preparing us for larger goals in the future.

Fear #2: Fear of Success
Here is failure's twin. The basis for this fear is pride in the results. Those who are captured by this fear are apprehensive about doing really well for fear of being held accountable in the future. Individuals with this fear often sabotage

their efforts by scattering their energy in too many directions at once. Leaving numerous incompletions in their trail, they justify their mediocre results by the rationale of "not enough time to get it all done!"

The way out: Turn the results of one's accomplishments over to life. If life works, and we allow life to work through us, we need not burden ourselves by taking personal pride in the results. Life is always successful and our job is to get out of the way and let life work through us. As we become conduits for life's energy rather than controllers, miraculous successes begin to occur all around us. Finally, when the goal is complete, we need only give credit where credit is due: to life itself!

Fear #3: Fear of Being Different

The fear of being different is held in place by the powerful influence of the pressure to conform. This peer pressure can drive people to sacrifice their individuality in favor of adopting the uniform attitudes and customs of the common majority, however arbitrary the common customs may be. This particular fear was often exhibited during our high school and college years and eventually it became an unconscious habit that began to run our behavior.

Again reframe the fear: We *are* different so let's begin to celebrate our differences. Every individual is a unique cell in the total body of mankind. It would be an unbalanced world if each cell in the world's body was exactly the same, with the same talents and gifts and the same inclinations! No one on earth will ever go through life your way.

The path of your life will not be like that of any other. Be willing to be who you are, and embrace your own life journey.

Fear #4: Fear of Change

I have discovered that the Comfort Zone fear, or fear of change, produces a form of paradigm paralysis. Patterns of thought and behavior become comfortable and what is comfortable becomes habit. Because any given system seeks to maintain equilibrium, and because the entire system has

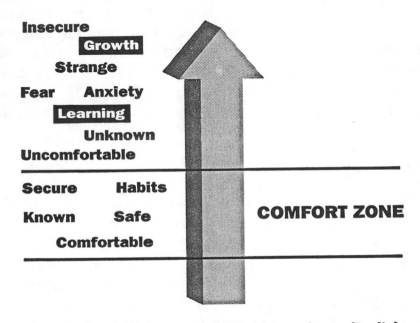

The Comfort Zone is our area of safety and security; it is made up of our old habits and the things that we know. It is only when we leave our C-Zone and enter the unknown that anxiety, insecurities and fears arise. The Catch 22 is that real learning and growth take place in the area of the unknown outside of our Comfort Zones. Therefore, opportunities for learning and growth are often accompanied by mixed emotions. When we enter the unknown and try something new we may experience everything from excitement and anxiety to out and out discomfort and fear. Even if the change is a healthy one, the emotions experienced during the learning and growth process are usually mixed.

to change when any part of it changes, old habits are often hard to alter regardless of whether or not they are healthy. Therefore, we often find ourselves clinging to old behaviors even though we know that these behaviors no longer support us.

There are definite stages to the process of making a change. In order to make change, learning and growth an ongoing part of our lives, we must understand these five stages so that we will not be caught off guard when they appear.

Stage 1: Denial

The first stage in making a change is often denial that there is any change to be made. A system at rest tends to remain at rest. In order to remain at rest, we often defend and justify the way we are while judging others who exemplify the new possibility. "I'm fine the way I am" is the central theme of this stage, and it's byline is, "but *that* is strange." In this stage the new possibility lies just beyond the power of our ability to imagine it for ourselves at that time.

Stage 2: Acceptance

If we continue to expose ourselves to the new idea or possibility, we eventually enter the Acceptance phase in the change process. This is a period of incubation; acceptance of the idea of change may occur quickly, or, as in the case of confronting a large change, it may take months to realize. In either case, we now value the change and view it as a positive choice. We have moved from rationalizing and justifying our position to considering the new possibility.

Stage 3: Willingness

With the advent of willingness we now perceive the change as a personal possibility. In this phase we have arrived at a new inner plateau in which the mind and heart are now willing to make a change. Ultimately, willingness is a prerequisite for any learning and growth; without our consent change becomes drudgery.

Stage 4: Decision

When we finally and fully accept the need to change and we are willing to do so, an inner call to action is heard and a decision for change ensues. Now the floodgate opens and the pent-up energy is released in the direction of the objective.

Stage 5: Action

At this point it is often best to advance out of our Comfort Zone one step at a time. However, many people, experiencing this pent-up surge of energy, go ripping out of their Comfort Zone zealously bound on achieving an instantaneous transformation not realizing that old habits run deep. Every living system, including our habit pattern system, seeks to maintain equilibrium, and if we push for a radical transformation, we do not allow the system time to rebalance throughout the change process.

In fact, the amount of resistance to change that we create will be equivalent to the distance and speed of the change, regardless of whether or not the change is good for us.

Resistance   Distance   Speed

The amount of resistance to change is equal to the distance that we travel out of our C-Zones plus the speed with which we execute the move; in other words, how far and how fast we leave our comfort zones.

In other words; **Resistance = Distance plus Speed** or **R=D+S**. People often give up because they thrust out of the Comfort Zone so fast and so far that the amount of resistance they create is too powerful for them to sustain the change. Result: They fall back into the safe and secure.

This can be exemplified in the story of a young woman who came to me with a desire to lose weight. She weighed about 170 pounds and although she was frustrated with her condition, she was deathly afraid of another failure. When I asked her what had happened, this was the story she told:

"I went on a diet twice last year and each time the pattern was similar. First, I made a decision to go on a strict diet and I felt really good about it. So I'd get up the next morning and have a cup of coffee and some juice. During my 10 a.m. work break I'd have a diet soda, still feeling really good about my decision. At lunch I'd have an apple and another diet soda, really excited that I was doing so well. By 3 p.m. I'd begin to feel weak. By 4 p.m. I'd be really hungry, and by 5 p.m. I'd arrive home totally ravenous. Each time I went straight to the refrigerator and gorged myself. The next day, I'd get up and start over. That would last for three or four days until I'd finally give up."

In this case, as in so many others, I recognized a classic case of R=D+S, and recommended a slow and steady change process over a radical transformation process.

This method is best expressed through the following story of a 76-year-old man who had just run his first marathon. When asked how he ever accomplished this feat, he replied: "In my early seventies I looked around me at all the young runners on the road and judged them. I thought that this running thing was a weird thing to do. (Stage 1) A few years later a lot of men and women of all ages had joined in the jog. Soon I found myself accepting the idea of running (Stage 2), and even wishing I were young enough to do it too. (Stage 3) Then I thought, Why not? If they can do it, I can do it too! (Stage 4)

"So I went to the running store and bought some brand new running shoes. (Begin Stage 5) But when I got them home, I found that I was just too scared to put them on. After all, I was 74 years old at that time and I had visions of dying of a heart attack out there."

He added, "For the first few days I left my shoes in the living room sitting right on the back of my couch. Every time I walked through the area I had to see them; I was mentally preparing myself to wear them. I'd even pick them up and get the feel of them and smell the brand new rubber and nylon. After awhile, when I was comfortable with their look and feel, I decided to try them on. For days I'd put them on and wander around the house with them, bouncing and springing and getting the feeling of wearing them. One day, I finally had an urge to go outside in my new shoes. So I sat on the curb and put them on and walked up and down the sidewalk. Finally, I began to lope down the street, only for a blocks at first, and then after a couple of weeks, I began going about a half a mile."

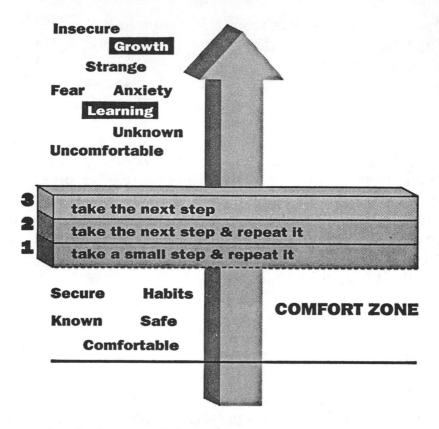

In order to accomplish any long range goal that is way out of your Comfort Zone, start by taking one small step at a time, and repeating it until it becomes comfortable. Once the behavior is stabilized, begin the process again by taking the next small step. Again repeat it until it feels comfortable. Patiently proceed with this 'one step at a time' process, and eventually, you will have gained a whole new behavior as well as expanded your Comfort Zone.

He looked at me with a twinkle in his eye and said, "It might seem like a long process, but it was sure worth it. I mean, no one who knew me then would have ever thought that this aging old man would ever complete a marathon. But I just did and, I did it one small step at a time!" (Completion of Stage 5)

There is great wisdom for all of us in this story. In order to accelerate the change process, we need only understand it and work with it.

Start to make a big change by taking a small step. Go just a small distance out of your Comfort Zones. (It may be uncomfortable but that's often the nature of change and growth!) Then repeat the small step again and again until it becomes comfortable. As soon as the behavior is stabilized and you have expanded your C-Zone just a bit, begin the process again by taking the next small step out. Again repeat it until it becomes comfortable. Eventually, you will have gained a whole new behavior.

ATTITUDINAL BLOCKS

Finally, we have the barriers of our own attitudes, assumptions, opinions and expectations. We often come into a learning situation loaded with preconceived notions about what it is that we expect to receive. As a result we often miss what is available.

Studies at various East Coast universities in the early 1980s reveal that the number one block to communication of any kind is judgment. How often do we find ourselves judging the person we are engaging with, or when we are at a seminar or lecture, judging the speaker or the speaker's style.

Due to recent brain research, we are beginning to understand why negative judgment is so detrimental to the learning process. The Reticular Activating System - known as the RAS - is a bundle of nerve fibers about the size of the tip of your finger located at the base of the brain stem. Its purpose as a regulator, is to filter incoming sensory information so that we don't go into sensory overload in any given moment. Working somewhat like a radio receiver, the RAS serves two specific functions. The first function is similar to the volume dial in that it controls the level of incoming information The second function is like the station control; it directs our attention by tuning in what we deem important and tuning out what we are not interested in at the moment.

It is the RAS that enables a mother to hear a change in her child's breathing in the middle of the night while other sounds go unnoticed. It is the RAS that allows us to focus our attention on a specific task at hand while tuning out sights and sounds extraneous to our immediate purpose.

Children with a damaged RAS are unable to focus their attention on any one thing at a time. They experience being totally bombarded by all the sights, sounds and sensations around them. Because of this constant bombardment, these children are unable to focus their attention long enough to hear what parents and teachers are saying. So acute was the result of a damaged RAS, that up until very recently, children suffering from major impairment of the RAS were thought to be mentally deranged. Recent brain research has helped isolate this condition as a physical phenomenon rather than a mental one.

In a normal functioning system, the RAS obeys the decisions made by the person living in the body suit. As an example of how this works, imagine two people arriving at 8:30 a.m. for a seminar. One was sent by his boss and doesn't want to be there, while the other eagerly anticipated the class. They spend the day sitting side by side in the same room learning the same material from the same instructor.

At the end of the day the person who didn't want to be there leaves declaring that his time was wasted because the instructor's voice was too loud, the lighting glared in the room, and the material was boring. The other person completes the day totally elated. He loved the instructor's vocal animation, thought that the material was fascinating, and was convinced it was the best use of his time and money.

What happened? It was the same event, the same instructor and the same material. The difference was the attitude of the individuals involved, and thus the direction in which the RAS of each was inclined. One RAS was told that the owner and operator of the body suit didn't want to be at the seminar while the other was told that its owner and operator was ecstatic to be there. Like the seek-and-search function on a car radio, each brain's filtering device spent the rest of the day gathering evidence that would make the individual operator of its body suit correct in his assumption.

It becomes obvious why judgment is detrimental to the learning process; our brain filters out anything that runs counter to our judgment and lets in anything that supports it. It is better to approach life as if we were a student and not an expert. It has been said that the expert knows many things and discovers few, while the student knows few things and discovers many. In other words, if we empty our mental cup and approach life without a lot of preconceived notions, we'll be more receptive to what is available in the moment.

Breaking Our Barriers

By now it is potently obvious that our mental attitude has a tremendous affect on our learning ability. Because of both our early childhood training and the attitudes and opinions we have stored about ourselves and others along the way, we have hampered the body suit's natural learning function. If we are to restore our body suit to its peak performance potential, we must begin by clearing past program deficiencies and establishing a prevailing set of inner conditions conducive to optimal receptivity.

BLOCKS AND BARRIERS	BREAKTHROUGHS
___ Fear of failure	All failures are really feedback. I learn from feedback and move on.
___ Fear of success	Every small success leads to a new success. I am learning and growing daily.
___ I'm not good enough	I am a fully capable person!
___ I can't get it; I'm not smart enough	If I apply myself, I can do anything.
___ Learning is boring	Learning is fun!
___ I get easily distracted	I'm learning to focus.
___ I'm too old to learn	There is no age limit on learning.

Review the preceding list of blocks and barriers, reframes and breakthroughs. Notice how we have countered each block and barrier with a powerful positive opposite. On a separate sheet of paper, list your own blocks to learning. Then ask yourself, *"What would an opposite belief be for that condition?"* As with the examples, list your positive opposites beside each of the blocks and barriers you listed. If you can't think of a powerful positive opposite that is believable to you, make up an answer; ask yourself. *"If there could be a powerful positive opposite, what would it be? What would it look or feel like?"*

Remember, most of our frustration with learning is a function of our beliefs, fears and attitudes about ourselves and our abilities. Just as logs that have jammed in the river reduce the flow of the current, so negative beliefs, fears, and attitudes reduce the internal electrical current of learning. As we reframe our thinking, we regain our freedom and enter a new land of learning where inspiration, insight, joy and enthusiasm are as natural as night and day.

POWER POINTS

❀

Our beliefs and attitudes shape our reality.

❀

I turn all mistakes into opportunities for
learning and growth.

❀

Judgment blocks learning.

❀

The amount of resistance to change is equal
to the Distance plus the Speed we travel out
of our Comfort Zone. R=D+S

❀

Expand your Comfort Zone one step at a time.

❀

Empty your mental cup.

❀

Reframe negative beliefs.

❀

Our performance potential is unlimited.

Chapter Three

MENTAL CLIMATE FOR OPTIMAL LEARNING

"The greater the joy within one's inner
consciousness, the greater the force of
the recharge of thought energy within..."

Walter Russell

The prevailing set of inner conditions within the mind
which enhance our learning will be referred to as the mental
climate for optimal learning. The backdrop for this climate
is a sky that is free from the cloud cover of anxiety, apprehension and strain. Tension and stress create toxins in the
system which reduce its ability to receive and dampen the
neuron firing in the brain.

The optimal mental atmosphere for learning is exhibited
by the young child. Trust, joy, spontaneity and exhilaration
are the inner states that children experience during learning. To the child, learning is neither a mental process nor
is it a conscious process. In fact learning for them is more
an event than a process. It is a joyous encounter with the

physical world; an encounter in which things are known by color, shape, sound, touch and feeling. It is an event in which pots and pans come to be known by size, shape and the sound they make when they are banged together or against something else.

Children lose themselves in play, and losing yourself in play is the essence of learning. Remember that child between the ages of birth and seven who we referred to earlier? That same child also learned to crawl, to walk, to manipulate his or her fingers and to feed himself. If you've ever watched your child or any child engaged in learning you become quickly aware of learning as an all consuming and exhilarating event. For a child, the process itself is fun!

Along with this we must not preclude the child's unfettered freedom from the fear of failure. Because learning is play and nothing is at stake when we play, there is no failure to a child; everything is discovery. *Mistakes are part and parcel of that discovery process; the "wrong" way is the avenue through which the "right" way is discovered.* Watch a child learning to walk; he falls and gets up dozens of times before mastering that first set of consecutive steps. As an adult, falling becomes a mistake, hence, it is that permission to make mistakes which becomes an essential ingredient in the adult learning process. I have often thought that it was a good thing we learned to walk early in life because our embarrassment at falling might have kept us from learning to walk in our later years!

We are not touting some naive return to innocence but rather an active synthesis of the child's joyful quest for knowledge as well as his natural acceptance of mistakes as part of that process. By turning learning into a game, by making it a playful event, we can begin to integrate the finely developed intellect of the adult with the awe that is experienced in youth. The world itself is a miraculous event, and there is something marvelous about our ability to engage with it, absorb it and learn from it.

When we harmonize the energies of joy, inspiration, wonder, spontaneity and a zest for discovery with the tremendous power of the adult intellect to concentrate and focus, learning shifts from separate and specific encounters to a continuous unfolding. The body suit is then freed to do what it does best: orchestrate this lifelong learning process by facilitating the flow of information through the channel of the senses along the neuron trails of least resistance into the folds and chambers of the brain for easy access when needed.

INCLUSIVE VS. EXCLUSIVE SORTING

During the course of the day our brain is constantly receiving information from its environment. This incoming information is continually being sorted at an unconscious level so that we can make sense out of our experience. This unconscious sorting process affects both our ability and the speed with which we are able to adapt, learn, change and grow. This internal and usually unconscious process is one of the most important determiners of whether we empower or disempower ourselves as learners.

I bumped into this realization as a result of many years of engaging with people in educational environments as well as in my personal life. Over time I began to notice a difference between those who learned rapidly and those who seemed to learn more slowly. As I began to study the differences in these two groups, I found that they appeared to receive information in two completely different ways.

Finally, I was able to locate the pulse of the difference and get my finger on it to test it. The heartbeat of the difference was the method by which each group sorted incoming information.

I have called these two methods exclusive and inclusive sorting. Exclusive sorting positions me, as the learner, separate from what I am learning and who I am learning from. Inclusive sorting, on the other hand, positions me "with" the incoming information and/or the person delivering that information. The group that learned slowly used an unconscious exclusive sorting method, while the group that learned quickly used an inclusive sorting method. The first approach, the method of exclusive sorting, seemed to disempower both the learner and the learning process, while inclusive sorting, seemed to empower the learner by opening the floodgates for learning.

By listening to the language he or she used to describe their experience I was finally able to locate an individual's internal process. Words such as *but, however* or *because* (with a negative attached) often reveal an unconscious exclusive sorting process. Exclusive sorting immediately precludes the possibility for rapid change or growth by defending the status quo. It often subtly rationalizes or justifies a position. For example:

That's possible for young people but I'm not young...
That's easy for her to do, because she is talented...
That's easy for you to say, but...
Oh sure, that works for you, but in my case....

Notice the power of shifting from an exclusive to an inclusive sorting procedure:

It's possible for young people and I'm young at heart...

If that's easy for her to do, then I can do it too..
That's easy for you to say, and for me too...
If it works for you, it will work for me....
In short, exclusive sorting separates us from the goal, while inclusive sorting makes the goal both conceivable and achievable. An example of a meta-inclusive sorting frame might be: *If it's possible in the world, it's possible for me!* When incoming information is received in this manner, we empower ourselves as capable of reaching for and achieving the objective.

A classic example of this is our receptivity toward Einstein. Most people view this genius through an exclusive sorting mechanism. "Well, Einstein was Einstein; he was special. He was different!" Inclusive sorting has a liberating effect, enabling the receiver to hold Einstein as a model of possibility rather than a reason for inadequacy. "If it was possible for Einstein to use his mental focus so potently, then it's possible for me to do the same!" This does not mean it's possible for me to be a great scientist, or to work in the area of physics, however, what this allows me to envision is the possibility of tapping a greater amount of my mental ability or my performance potential.

After all, isn't that what Einstein really represents, an unobstructed personality set free from the fetters of limitation? The real question is, "What can I learn from a man like Einstein?" and only via the mechanism of inclusive sorting can we follow the trail of that question to its ultimate conclusion, the awakening of our own inner potential and the fulfillment of our own life's promise.

EXPANSIVENESS

Expansiveness is the climatic aspect that establishes the

condition for steady growth, increase and inclusiveness. *Expansiveness is to learning fitness as what adding more weights on the barbell is to muscle fitness.* Expansiveness is the opposite of contraction; like the open-ended universe, it extends the boundaries of our solar system to the galaxies beyond. It is progressive, productive and energetic with an emotional undertone characterized by a spirited enthusiasm for life and a zest for learning.

We can best comprehend the power of this mental state by observing its interaction with the world. An expansive mind encounters new ideas or concepts willingly. Even if the thought seems to run counter to the already accepted body of knowledge of the receiver, the expansive mind will make room for it. It may not immediately act on the information, but the critical key is that it will not foreclose on it. Rather, it will take the new information and put it on a holding shelf until further incoming data elucidates it, counters it, or accents its meaning.

Inclusiveness and expansiveness may be the most important mental states we can develop in our children, for they will be indispensable conditions for the 21st century. As we move toward an international community and a shared body of knowledge, each one of us will be asked to expand to include cultural differences. A natural distillation will occur as each culture pours forth into the new world stream and the finest from each blends into a new world order.

POSSIBILITY VS. PROBABILITY

Another critical variation in the mental climate which empowers or disempowers the learning process is that of probability vs. possibility. Probability thinkers create their future by using references from the past. A probability mentality depends on data and information from past experience to predict the outcome of a present or future situation. In other words, *probability creates the future out of the past.* Given that our past experience of learning often left us dysfunctional, using probability as a frame of reference for our future learning will often create a dysfunctional future.

In order to establish a mental environment that opens us to our true performance potential, we need only develop a domain of possibility. Establishing a climate of possibility is a creative act: Depending upon nothing from the past, it asserts itself as a whole new way and thrusts us out beyond the horizon of certainty. There is no certainty in a universe of creation. It is a willingness to live creatively without the support of evidence. All massive scientific breakthroughs and all innovative discoveries have been born out of the womb of possibility. The seed of a quantum leap can only be nourished in the fertile womb that possibility makes available.

Like changing the train track we're riding on, possibility can change the direction of our entire future. The application of this concept has proven to be an extremely potent aspect of my work. It created miracles at the women's prison in Oahu by derailing women from their past, setting them on a track of healing, and thrusting them forward on their learning journey. At the organizational level, possibility has allowed me to innovatively engage in the creation of learning organizations based on trust, support, and teamwork. Viewing life through the lens of possibility has also allowed me to initiate leading edge exploration into the possibility that family training may provide. To date those organizations which are offering training for spouses, children and parents of staff members have been thrilled with the results of bringing education to their loved ones.

All of this is derived from the application of "The Possibility Factor" as we sometimes call it. Probability limits, while possibility frees; probability binds, while possibility liberates; probability restrains, while possibility releases. *Creating an inner climate of possibility is a compelling response to a personal or cultural history founded on limitations and distortions. Where probability would have recreated that past in the present moment, possibility unshackles us and allows a present and future of our own choosing.*

ATTITUDINAL SETS

While inclusivity and possibility are the prevailing conditions necessary for optimal learning, I have found the following to be the specific mental attitudes necessary for achieving our full performance potential. Webster says that attitude is "the leaning of the mind," and I have found several attributes that enhance and accelerate every student's learning journey.

Ganus

Ganus is a Spanish word that comes from a Latin root; to have the ganus is to have the desire or passion for.... anything. Ganus covers a myriad of emotions from willingness to fervor, from enthusiasm to zeal. To have the ganus is to have the spirit, the desire, the will, the fire, the craving, the hunger, the yearning, and the aspiration all rolled up in one. Ganus is the fuel for learning. Ganus propels the child forward in his discovery process for it ignites and sustains his interest in his world.

Ganus is a critical requisite for the achievement of our performance potential because without it we will find ourselves hard pressed to sustain our commitment when we hit a bump or a turn on the path of achievement. Ganus renews our energy nourishing our hope and faith, and fueling the fire necessary to pursue our long-term goals. Without the ganus the well spring of our energy and vitality will run dry. With the ganus, the fire of our desire will be constantly rekindled as we move toward the accomplishment of our goals.

Open-mindedness

An open mind is like an open door. To have an open mind is to keep one's mental door open to any and all possibilities that avail themselves. Open-mindedness acknowledges and allows for the flow of life while establishing the mental climate necessary to learn from the incidents and events that transpire on a daily basis. It is in some way similar to expansiveness in that it predisposes us to being responsive and receptive to new information, new ways and new opportunities.

Permission

As noted earlier, permission means allowing ourselves to make mistakes and to learn and grow from those mistakes rather than beating ourselves up over them. Permission is a key ingredient in our transformation. Without it we would miss the fundamentals and incapacitate our present abilities. Just as we couldn't imagine learning to stand, walk or talk for the first time without permission to make mistakes: it's hard to imagine learning to ride a bike or swim or skate without any mistakes.

Most people quit giving themselves permission somewhere in their early teens when peer pressure sets in. It wasn't acceptable to make mistakes in our teens, and its definitely not OK to make certain mistakes at thirty or forty! Imagine a 30- or 40-year-old trying to learn to ride a bike without training wheels. Their first bike experience might go something like this: He or she gets on the bike expecting to ride on the first try. "Oops!" They go a few feet and fall off saying, "Oh, that was silly!" Then looking around the person continues," I hope nobody saw me do that," and finally the scene closes with, "That was stupid! I'll never try that again!"

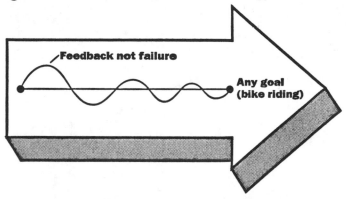

In our new learning model mistakes are a way of learning, not the end result of learning badly. Turning all small failures into feedback and all feedback into learning. By a series of course corrections we eventually arrive at the goal.

Let us turn small failures into learning opportunities. As in the case of our bike-riding example, we often learn by a series of mistakes and adjustments. Sometimes our best feedback comes from our greatest mistakes.

Beginning today, when you are in a new situation make allowances for learning and adjustment. As you will discover in the following chapters, this includes time for sleep and relaxation. Learning is not always a conscious process, much of it occurs at the subliminal level where the neuro-physiological mechanisms of the body-mind have time to synthesize and integrate the material from our daily experience. The mental atmosphere for optimal learning must include permission to make mistakes, the willingness to gain the feedback from those mistakes, and time to make the necessary adjustments for success. As we give ourselves permission and recommit to the goal, we actually accelerate our learning effectiveness.

OPTIMAL MENTAL CLIMATE FOR LEARNING

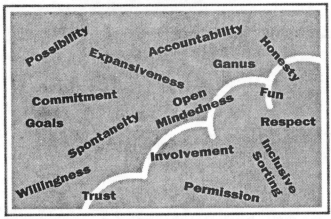

Periodically clouds may arise in your mental sky. Imagine the wind blowing them away, or imagine yourself catching them and throwing them into the rubbish where they dissolve. Either way, consciously release them and refocus on your learning goal.

Well that's all great but....

What happens if we begin to have a reaction or judge someone? We're human and we're not totally in control of our reactions. What if we begin to close down? What if we suddenly find that we are not being open-minded? The diagram shows the perfect mental climate for optimal accelerated learning. However, it is obvious that a mental climate is not a static condition! What do I do if a cloud drifts in?

Good question! Let's say you're in a learning situation. You've decided to take a class on computer technology. Excited to have an opportunity to practice your new learning skills, you arrive at class early and position yourself in the front row. Anticipation heightens as you observe the trainer enter the room and set up the overhead projector. Then he opens his mouth and the nasal pitch drives you crazy. You begin to judge his twang, and as you do, suddenly everything about him bothers you. His walk, mannerisms, and the sound of his voice blend into a total irritation and you find yourself closing down.

STOP! Remember what happens to the RAS on your body suit when you close someone out! *Remember to remember* that you are a being and that you have a choice! Stop action on the movie! Find the nearest rubbish can, crumple your judgment up into a ball and throw it in. If it's hard to let go of the judgment, tell yourself that you can pick it up when you leave and take it home with you.

I've shared this technique often and most people tell me that by the time the day is over they've completely forgotten about the judgment. They became absorbed in the day, time flew and they learned a lot.

As you can see, creating an optimal mental climate for learning is an active, process-oriented adventure that will engage every aspect of your awareness as a human being. Learning is the central feature of living rather than a peripheral event and as the joy of our own personal learning journey unfolds we will begin to experience the superlative powers of the body suit's natural ability to absorb its environment.

As we release ourselves from the chains and fetters of limiting mental attitudes we shall once more discover our own inherent brilliance.

POWER POINTS

❀

The optimal mental climate for learning includes
trust, joy, optimism, spontaneity and exhilaration.

❀

In our new learning to learn model, mistakes are part
of the learning process. The "wrong" way is the
avenue through which the "right" way is discovered.

❀

Inclusive sorting makes our goal
conceivable and achievable.

❀

If it is possible in the world it is possible for me.

❀

Creating an inner climate of possibility unshakles
us from our past and allows us to create
a future of our own choosing.

❀

Ganus is the fuel for learning. To have the ganus is
to have the spirit, the desire, the will, the fire,
the craving, the hunger, the yearning and
the inspiration all rolled up in one.

❀

As we release ourselves from the chains and fetters
of limiting mental attitudes, we shall once more
discover our own inherent brilliance.

Chapter Four

THE INFINITE MIND:
EXPLORING UNIVERSES WITHIN

"It is not clear that there are any limits to the human mind other than those we believe in."

Willis Harman

While physicists are traversing the land of quarks and astronomers are probing the deepest reaches of infinite space, another group of scientists has turned its attention to universes within. Although the territories are different, the similarities between them are fascinating.

Here in the language of electrical impulses, neurochemicals, neurotransmitters, neuropeptides, dendrites, synapses and neurons, these scientists are unlocking the secrets of the human body suit and its central control system, the brain. As new frontiersmen, they are beginning to describe a world of interactive processes much like that of the atomic universe. To these contemporary investigators, perceptions are experienced as biological waves of energy. In this new territory scientists describe a world where sights, sounds, feelings and ideas are translated into biochemical processes that sweep through the brain and body.

Research pouring forth from these intriguing laboratories of neuroscience indicate that the capacity of the human brain and body is seemingly infinite. At the same time, researchers have discovered the inaccuracy and unfairness of standard IQ testing. Thus far, they have identified seven different types of intelligences: interpersonal, introspective, spatial, bodily, musical, verbal and mathematical. This information will ultimately revolutionize our lives as radically as Galileo's and Copernicus' discoveries revolutionized life in the 16th and 17th centuries.

In this new era, it will come to be irrevocably accepted by the mass of society that, given a normal healthy body suit, any limitation in our capacities is self-created. With these new realizations will come greater accountability. Human beings will begin to realize their responsibility for the care and sustenance of their brains as well as the care and sustenance of their physical bodies.

BRAIN CHALLENGE: THE EVIDENCE

Evidence suggests that the more we challenge our brains and push them to expand, the greater their capacity for expansion. On the other hand, if we avoid mental challenges we stunt our brain's capacity for greater challenges in the future. In fact, reports indicate that the more we learn the more we are capable of learning, and the more we commit to memory, the greater our capacity for memory becomes.

In laboratory results throughout the world, the implications are clear; *the brain is like a muscle.* We can develop superior abilities by pushing our brain, stimulating it, forcing it to think, pressing it to stretch, expand and grow beyond its C-Zone.

Research also denotes the inaccuracy of the assumption that the brain reaches maturity and then stops growing. In the past, regeneration of brain cells and expansion in the size of the brain were thought of as impossible. In his book *MEGABRAIN*, Michael Hutchison reports that given the right stimulation, regeneration of at least one type of brain cell can occur, and that whether we are ages 30, 50, or 80, if we challenge our brains they will continue to grow with stimulation. The neurological connections in the brain get richer as we age.

From all indications, the Eastern traditions may have been correct when they honored their elders as wise beings in the apex of their lives. Is it possible that we in the West will someday learn from our Eastern ancestors? As we become more responsible for developing ourselves both mentally as well as physically we may discover for ourselves the joy and wisdom available in a long and gracious aging process.

OUR LIVES AS LABORATORIES

As human beings, complete with body and a brain, we have an opportunity to compile our own research within the private laboratories of our lives. I committed myself to my own personal research program years ago, and since that time, my life has become a learning adventure.

About thirteen years ago my personal research program accelerated drastically when it was suggested that I read *The Tao of Physics* by Fritjof Capra. The suggestion came at the close of a rigorous day of training from a young participant.

Standing in front of me was a trainee, smiling and anxious to share something special. For him it was an intimate moment, while for myself, I was suddenly catapulted into a violent inner reaction. I tried to remain calm and unfettered on the outside so that my exterior posturing would not reveal what I was experiencing, but my mind was reeling within. "Read a physics book?!! You must be crazy; I hate physics so much that I even avoided taking it in high school."

I couldn't believe what I was hearing. My inner dialogue sounded like a committee of justifiers; all the defenders of the status quo had risen up within me! Suddenly, as I viewed the inner and outer scene the whole situation became laughable. I was inwardly feeling as if he was the prosecuting attorney and I was the defendant. At that moment, my still small voice became audible beneath the din of my justifications. "It sounds like you're a hypocrite; how can you possibly teach people to break through their limited beliefs and get out of their Comfort Zones if you aren't willing to get out of yours? You'd better go after it because if you buy into your limitations and reasons, you'll never be able to teach what you teach."

I thanked the young man in front of me for in an instant he had unknowingly allowed me to experience a powerful mental barrier and process myself all the way through it. I left the workshop that day promising him that I would buy the book and read it, and I truly meant it.

Two days later I purchased *The Tao of Physics*. When I first took it off the bookshelf, I remember thinking I'd never get through it. It seemed like a large volume, more than 300 pages of sheer intellect, or so I thought. The book was so overwhelming that it sat unopened on the coffee table in my living room for a few days.

But my most powerful memory of the event of the book was the first few hours that I spent with it. I must have read the initial pages four or five times with no understanding whatsoever of what I was reading. I kept going back to the beginning and starting over as my mind drifted in and out, decidedly trying to get away from the task that I had put before it.

Finally, I firmly resolved to "get it," and as I did, my inner responses changed. My breathing slowed to a near standstill and everything grew still within me as I focused in on the sentence before me. Then my body relaxed and I gently directed my mind as an inner voice stilled my awareness. It was as if I could hear the voice whispering inwardly, "Shh, stay with it; you can get it." Quietly and slowly I read the first page again, then one more time very slowly. I began to experience a deep stillness, and as I did the reading became easier. This time, every time I re-read it, I absorbed more.

This little-by-little awakening continued over three or four readings and then something marvelous happened. It was as if a veil was ripped away. I plummeted into the text. The words came to life before my eyes. Every phrase became startlingly electric as I suddenly understood what moments before had looked like Greek to me.

I was mesmerized. The cocoon had suddenly snapped and the butterfly was now testing new wings, catapulted out of an old mental model into a vast and infinitely mysterious domain in which physics and philosophy merged. I was learning to fly, soaring out of the known universe into a galaxy of strange proportions and dimensions. Like a hungry child that had discovered a new food, I found myself devouring the entire book in three days. A week later I discovered that I was being enigmatically drawn back to the physics section of the bookstore. In the second stage of this new hunger, I consumed *The Dancing Wu Li Masters* by Gary Zukav. Later, I went on to explore a multitude of books in the area of the new physics.

I hope that the young man who instigated that event reads this book someday, and that when he does, he remembers the role he played. A multitude of gifts issued forth from

Process + Product = Outcome

Process is the 'how' of learning; it is the way we go about learning. Product is the 'what' of learning; it is the material or curriculum we are working with. The outcome is the end result and it includes both the skills (such as focus) and character abilities (such as patience) developed in the process, as well as the material or the product learned. Often the benefits achieved in the process are just as valuable, if not more valuable, to the goal of life-long learning than is the product. As we learn 'how' to learn, we can choose any 'what' to learn.

that single act of sharing with me that day. In truth, what transpired from that short conversation changed my life forever.

The first two benefits came from the process itself. First, I began to observe my reactions (as exemplified in the thoughts and feelings I had when the trainee was sharing the title of the book with me), not as if they were me, but as if they were simply reactions. I began to see myself as separate from and bigger than my reactions, and I began to quicken my ability and expand my learning by going beyond my reactions.

Secondly, I reclaimed an infinitely powerful ability when I learned to "stay with it until I got it." This ability to enter a slow-motion state, stilling my mind and concentrating on the task at hand, has proven to be one of my greatest gifts. To this day I utilize it when I'm speaking to a large group or when I'm preparing material for seminars. It is this ability that allows me to tune in and get the answers I need or retrieve a piece of information from memory. I have also taught many of my students to utilize this method of focused stillness to enhance both memory and understanding.

The third and forth benefits were noted in the outcome. The first was a bit of well-needed humility born of the realization that if Planet Earth is really a classroom then those who come to us are our teachers along the way. People in our lives are life's messengers and as we learn to listen to them we can often discover the next lesson needed for our development. From that moment on I developed a willingness to really listen and learn from those who came to me knowing that they might hold a necessary key for my advancement.

The final gift from all of this was the gift of expanded awareness. My consciousness was never the same from that day forth. In fact, it was completely transformed. It was as if my intellectual capacity had been amplified and expanded a hundred-fold. Like a rubber band, it had been stretched to a new capacity and it would never snap back to its old shape again.

As an off-shoot, I learned that *intellect is elastic* and that it can be stretched and expanded. This knowledge and the practice of pushing my mind to expand has continued to this day.

Naturally, I gained from the product or the curriculum involved here. In other words, I garnered a wealth of information about the merger of physics and philosophy.

Although the knowledge was very exciting to me, it is interesting to note that what stayed with me over time were the benefits received from the process and the outcome. The real benefits from the incident were beyond the domain of curriculum.

It seems to me that it is this way in our educational system also. The real learning that took place for me in school was often peripheral. As a student I learned as much, if not more, from the character and delivery of my teachers then from the curriculum itself.

Today, in dealing with hundreds of teachers seeking to inspire their students, I would surmise that the process of education is at least as critical, if not more critical, than the product. Ultimately, the product will change. Physics for example, will continue to grow as a science. Textbooks will have to adapt to include the expanding body of knowledge. But the peripheral learning that occurs as a result of an inspiring teacher using enthusiasm and love to deliver the curriculum never leaves us.

Hopefully we will pay more attention to the process of learning in the future for learning to learn is about this very process. By teaching our children *how* to learn, the *what* of learning will become easy.

POWER POINTS

✿

Intellect is elastic; it can be stretched and expanded. The more we learn the greater our capacity for learning.

✿

Our life is our private laboratory for learning.

✿

We reclaim an infinitely powerful ability when we learn to "stay with it" until we get it.

✿

Process + Product = Outcome

✿

As we pay attention to the process of learning, learning becomes easier.

✿

As we begin to see ourselves as separate from and bigger than our reactions, we quicken and expand our ability to learn.

✿

Planet Earth is a classroom and those who come to us are our teachers along the way.

Chapter Five

RELAXATION AND HIGHER-ORDER THINKING

> "I am convinced that to act effectively
> we must know the how and why of
> things. Otherwise we grope our way,
> going around in circles and getting lost.
> If our will to make progress, and the
> motivations that underlie our effort, do
> not rest on a strong enough foundation,
> we may break down along the way!"
>
> Monique Le Poncin

For more than twenty years now information has been pouring in from brain laboratories all over the world regarding the differences between stress and relaxation in relationship to the learning process. These studies have revealed a vast amount of information regarding the nature of the relationship between our body's automatic responses and learning. In general, these studies reveal that neither stress nor anxiety are conducive to higher-order thinking, for they alter the flow of information both to and within the brain.

Because we are living in an extremely stressful period in history, this research directly affects each and every one of us. What *exactly* happens when we are stressed out? As we start to understand our body suit's automatic responses, we can then learn to regulate them in order to achieve optimal performance.

The Fight or Flight Response

Over the long and ancient history of human development, the human body evolved an extremely fast and effective reflex system for dealing with perceived environmental threats. This system, called the fight or flight response, instantaneously mobilizes all of our physical energies in order to either fight the sensed threat or run from it. In other words, it mobilizes our body's energies for external activity.

When something threatens or scares us our bodily reactions are both immediate and instinctive. Neurochemicals are released in the brain to mobilize energy; and the brain's electrical activity shifts to beta waves which is indicative of external focus and activity. Glucose (sugar) then floods into the system, the heart rate accelerates and blood is diverted from the brain, digestive system and periphery of the body to the heart and trunk muscles. Breathing accelerates and oxygen consumption increases. As the body's blood pressure rises sweating increases.

This tremendous concentration of energy known as the "adrenaline rush" is a perfect survival mechanism for a species in that it mobilizes the entire system for immediate and powerful physical activity. The fight or flight response is an excellent answer to dealing with physical threats such

71

as charging elephants or hungry tigers. However, its effect on logical, or higher-order thinking is fatal.

Research also notes that the brain constitutes about 2 percent of our total body weight but it only utilizes about 20 percent of our body's total oxygen supply. However, when oxygen and blood are shunted away from the brain, our brain simply does not function as well. Our responses often become clumsy, if not totally inept! Normally effective people have been known to function extremely ineffectively under high stress.

All of us have had an experience similar to this at one time or another. Whether in a business meeting or on the golf course, tension has an adverse effect on our ability to focus and, therefore, on our results. Most of us remember what it was like to be anxious during a school or college test and the effect this had on our performance.

To this day, young people in our school systems report that they often don't do as well under stressful test conditions. In short, stress has a calamitous effect on the workings of the brain and on our ability to think quickly. The body's natural learning ability is disabled.

Because of the complexity of the times in which we live and the constant daily tensions that ensue, many of us live in a continual state of non-specific low-grade arousal. In other words, we tend to be slightly stressed all the time. This incessant low-grade stress is detrimental to normal healthy mental functioning. Because of this state of consistent slight arousal, most people never become aware of their optimal learning abilities. In other words, an abnormal state has become normal, and this poses a critical problem for anyone whose goal is to achieve their performance potential.

The Relaxation Response

Until recently, very few people have been aware that the body has another instinctive function that is completely opposite of the fight or flight response. While the fight or flight response mobilizes our body's energies for external activity, the "relaxation response," as it was labeled by Dr. Herbert Benson of Harvard Medical School, mobilizes our body's resources for internal activity. In other words, the relaxation response enhances our ability to receive information by mobilizing the bodies resources for heightened inner awareness, and therefore, for learning.

The effects of the relaxation response are the exact opposite of the effects of the flight response. The brain's electrical activity drops from beta to alpha or theta. Brain wave patterns in left and right hemispheres synchronize, the heart rate slows, blood pressure drops and muscles become relaxed. Therefore, the amount of blood and oxygen going to the brain increases.

Research has systematically and conclusively shown that the relaxation response relieves stress as well as anxiety, which is a symptom of stress. It therefore, ameliorates the condition of constant low-grade arousal. It appears that the normal learning function of our body suit is rehabilitated during the relaxation response.

Focusing and the "Felt -Shift" Experience

Finally, let's take a closer look at one of the primary distinctions between the fight or flight response and the relaxation response: the difference in the brain's activity during each state. During deep relaxation the brain's energy goes through a rapid permutation or change and this change seems to be conducive to the "Aha" experience and the instant understanding that accompanies it. Researchers have found that this experience seems to occur when we enter the "theta" range of brain wave activity and it is closely linked to hemispheric synchronization. (See appendix)

Eugene Gendlin, author of *Focusing*, describes a technique of withdrawing the attention inward and focusing on a problem that you are trying to solve. Rather than dealing with the problem directly, Gendlin's students are taught to "center" or still the mind through a series of focusing steps. Stilling the mind and emotions allows one to understand the problem. A "felt-shift" is then experienced, marked by a sudden tension release coupled with instant clarity in which the entire solution to the problem crystallizes and is totally understood.

Gendlin, with the use of EEG readings, discovered that this "felt-shift" experience was matched by a sudden drop into the lower alpha state or upper theta brain wave state. Somehow, it is this alteration in brain waves that brings with it the well known "Aha" or "Eureka" awakening so often spoken of as part of the creative experience. This "felt-shift" either brings about or reflects a reordering at higher integrative levels.

As I read Gendlin's material about four years after my "Tao" experience, I suddenly understood what had occurred in those moments of staying with it while reading those first few pages of the "Tao" book over and over. I had been centering for some time prior to picking up *The Tao of Physics*, and I recognized the telltale physical signals described by Gendlin. As I told myself to "stay with it; you can get it," a deep stillness came over me, my mind became one-pointed and my breathing slowed almost to a standstill as I focused deeply. Then I suddenly plummeted into the altered awareness described by Gendlin in which I instantly understood the entire text.

EDUCATIONAL IMPLICATIONS

This theta range of activity in which the brain is functioning as an integrated structure seems to hold a miraculous key to the secrets of learning to learn. Here we achieve hemispheric synchronization, as indicated when both hemispheres are generating the same brain waves at the same time and the corpus callosum is firing, exchanging information rapidly between the two.

Furthermore, the theta range with its distinctive property of hemispheric synchronization appears to result in some very impressive learning features. In this state whole brain sensory integration is high and people report a peak experience feeling. Receptivity to visualization is also extremely high in the theta range, and people report that they have vivid memory recall as well a heightened ability to generate new ideas.

Obviously the potential for optimal learning is extremely high in the theta range. Thus, it may hold a key to the accelerated and innovative learning necessary to solve the financial, ecological and social challenges that our generation and those to come are now facing.

Educators, psychologists and scientists involved in brain research are currently investigating techniques to assist people in entering this state where learning seems to happen easily and where the processing and storage of information seems to occur at lightning speed.

At "The Academy," our eight-month training program for community leaders and business people, we have integrated many of the new techniques now being explored as part of our course curriculum. Guided imagery, centering, body movement, dance, exercise, speech delivery, the study of language, and deep relaxation are some of the techniques included. Work, play and humor are combined to release the latent potential available in each student. People are also taught to utilize and integrate enhanced awareness states in conjunction with business skills, incorporating tools such as mind mapping, power planning, and power note-taking skills (Section 2).

Naturally, our Academy graduates are ecstatic about the results they are experiencing in their lives, for the effects of this work defy normal educational standards. Who among us can calibrate the power of the infinite mind? Human beings who come to truly understand the correct function and use of their body suits begin to perform exquisitely. Once the portal to their full performance potential has been cleared they discover that behind it lies an infinite set of possibilities.

Each Academy graduate determines these possibilities for himself by the nature of his or her own personal goals and gifts. Yet, each reports that the results of body-mind integration in the context of proper state-of-the-art training have released them to perform at higher levels than ever before imagined. Personal and business relationships blossom, productivity increases and the clutter of everyday living becomes din in the glow of growth. The transformation is well under way. Remember to remember...life works, get out of the way and let it.

What does it mean to be a human being? It means that we have been given a body suit specifically constructed for rapid integrative learning. We need only discover how to use our suits appropriately and wisely for they were designed to support us in learning what we need to learn so that we may accomplish our lifetime goals.

Educators are standing on a precipice overlooking a new universe. The learning laboratories of the future will include an understanding of the workings of the human body and mind. These teachers will serve as models and guides for the youth in our communities, for in coming to understand themselves, they will become adept at assisting others in similar understanding. The teachers of the future will be students of life, well skilled in the art of using their own personal lives as laboratories for learning.

POWER POINTS

❀

The body's natural learning ability is
disabled by stress.

❀

The fight or flight response mobilizes our body's
energies for external activity.

❀

The relaxation response mobilizes the body's
energies for internal activities and
learning is an internal activity.

❀

The theta brain range holds a key to
the secrets of rapid learning.

❀

Throw open the gateway to your full performance
potential, for behind it lies infinite
performance possibilities.

Chapter Six

CENTERING AND OUR PERFORMANCE POTENTIAL

"From the center where the Will of God is known. Let purpose guide the little wills of men."

The Great Invocation
Alice Bailey

As we discovered in the previous chapter most of us are living a majority of the time in a state of constant low-grade arousal. In other words, the relaxation response doesn't happen spontaneously in the everyday accelerated pace of our Western culture. Furthermore, the ability to induce the relaxation response is a requisite for higher-order thinking and ultimately the achievement of our performance potential.

My own discoveries in this regard occurred as a result of one of the primary relationships of my youth. My grandfather, on my father's side of the family, came to the Hawaiian Islands as a plantation manager in the early 1900s. He lived with my grandmother on the Big Island for many years where he encountered the teachings of the Eastern tradition. In his late thirties grandfather became a Buddhist priest and by the time I was born almost thirty years later, he had been meditating for more than one hour a day for over thirty years.

As a child who was raised in the Christian tradition, I never really understood what made grandfather different. But indeed, I did know that there was something very special about him. While grandfather was extremely alert and mentally active, a deep stillness seemed to emanate from his body; it was as if peace surrounded him. Grandfather never missed a beat. Active yet still, vibrant yet peaceful, he was able to accomplish more than the average individual during his ninety-year-span on the planet.

As a young girl, I was not cognizant of all of this. I only knew that grandfather's energy was different. He was unlike any person I had ever met. It was not until much later in life, through my own direct experience of centering that I became aware of the connection between higher-order thinking and expanded awareness and the active stillness I had experienced in my grandfather's presence.

It is at this point that all logical discourse on the power and value of centering is thrown to the wind. In retrospect, as I stand on the edge of the plateau overlooking the hills and valleys of my life, centering lies at the midpoint of the terrain. Like the maypole that pulls seemingly fragmented energies into a unified whole, centering is the middle pole connecting the apparently disjointed aspects of consciousness thus giving coherence to the entire field of one's awareness.

Centering is to the achievement of our performance potential as food is to the life of our body.

   Although centering does not deliver startling or immediate results, it is a practice in which the process and product
merge and a permutation of consciousness ensues. As one
consistently continues in the daily practice, a quiet discipline and sense of stillness develops within. In time, a
subtle and deep transition occurs as normal awareness is
altered and heightened states are achieved.
   If the mind could be compared to a mighty ocean, then
thoughts would be like waves cresting on its surface. During
normal awareness we know only the surface waves; thoughts
splashing one upon another as awareness is buffeted from
one idea and emotion to the next. As we learn to center, we
begin to dive deep beneath the surface cresting of our
mental sea into the depths of the stillness where inner
knowing is encountered. With long-term practice, the
agitations of the restless mind are stilled, a continuity of
consciousness emerges as insight and intuition fuse on the
field of intellect, and perception is transformed.
   With a bit of practice each of us can master the basics of
centering, an adaptation of what I learned from grandfather. I have shared this particular technique with hundreds
of students, finding it to be one of the easiest methods that
I know of for stilling the activity of the restless mind.
However talking about centering to someone who has never
experienced it is like talking to an alien about water. Just as
the alien would need to taste and perhaps bathe in water to
"get it" so centering must be experienced to be understood.
Thus, the accelerated learning audio cassette series that was
created to accompany this book, takes you though the step-
by-step process which follows.

Centering Cues
   Imagine trying to balance on one foot. As you try a few

times, you will finally notice that focusing on a spot on the horizon makes it much easier to balance. Similarly, centering becomes easier when we focus our inner attention on something in order to still the agitations of the restless mind. To do this we will use the rise and fall of our own breath as it enters and ebbs from our body combined with visual, auditory, and kinesthetic or emotional feeling cues.

VISUAL CUE: A vibrant yellow-white light

AUDITORY CUE: A word or phrase of your own choosing such as peace or love

KINESTHETIC CUE: Feel the tranquility that your words bring

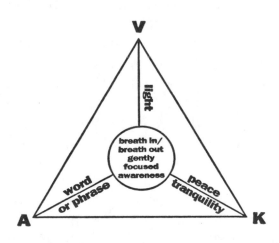

The key to centering lies in harnessing the inner visual, auditory, and kinesthetic channels of awareness. As we quiet the inner senses we enter the stillness to find a peace that surpasses understanding.

Choosing Your Centering Word or Phrase
Begin by choosing a word or phrase that has a peaceful, quieting effect on you. Most of our students share that certain phrases from their own spiritual tradition seem to have a natural stilling effect on their minds. Christians often use words such as Lord, God or Heavenly Father or a phrase from the Book of Psalms in the Bible. In the Hindu tradition words such as Om or Shanti (which means peace) appear to instill tranquility. Shalom might be used for the Jewish tradition, or Buddha for the Buddhist tradition. Those who are not of a specific spiritual background have chosen words such as peace, tranquility, stillness, joy, love, or any phrase that has a peaceful effect on them.

Remember that the theta brain wave state is not compatible with feelings of stress. Therefore, pick a word or phrase that will enhance your sense of calmness and inner peace. This will make it is easy for your mind to internalize the feelings of stillness and serenity desired. For many, a comfortable word or phrase will be automatic. However, don't worry if a word or phrase doesn't come to you immediately. Take your time in choosing one.

Once your word or phrase has been chosen, stay with it, for, over time, it will become the anchor in your mental sea, predisposing the mind to stillness as soon as you give the word attention.

Centering Exercise
STEP 1:
Sit in a comfortable position with your spine erect against the back of the chair or couch. Continue

83

with your own sitting style if you already meditate.

STEP 2:
Close your eyes, breathe and feel the gentle rise and fall of your own chest as you take a moment to reflect on *who you really are.* Say to yourself, "I am a being wearing a physical body while I am here on Earth."

STEP 3:
As you slow your breathing, visualize a vibrant orb of yellow-white light about the size of a baseball at the heart level in the center of your chest. Feel the warmth of the light permeating your chest and experience the peace, radiance and cleansing effect of that light as it pours through your body. Bask in this feeling for a few moments as a sense of quiet relaxation flows through the body.

STEP 4:
Now visualize the light moving up to the center of your forehead between the eyebrows. Stabilize your visual awareness on the light, and feel the inner stillness

and peace that floods the head as you focus your visual awareness on the light.

STEP 5:
Continue to see and feel the light as you inhale slowly and then exhale saying your word or phrase on the incoming and outgoing breath. As you say your word or phrase inwardly, use the full round of your inhalation and/or exhalation for the repetition.

Examples:
If you chose a phrase, inhale as you say half of the phrase to yourself and exhale as you say the other half.
Inhale: Our Father / Exhale: which art in heaven

If you have chosen two words such as "Peace, Love", the method is the same. Inhale: Peace / Exhale: Love.

If you have chosen a single word, inhale with your attention on the breath; then repeat your word during the exhalation.

STEP 6:
As thoughts arise during this process, imagine that they are like birds flying through your mental sky. Release them, let them fly while you gently bring

85

your attention back to the flood
of light in your mental sky and to
your centering word or phrase
when it rides in and out on the
tide of the breath.

STEP 7:
Continue for 10 to 15 minutes
once or twice a day.

(In our training, we refer to centering as the "inner work." I recommend that beginners start their inner work by centering for just 15 minutes a day, five days a week so as not to go too far out of the Comfort Zone. After one month increase centering time to 20 minutes a day five days a week. Stabilize there until you desire to expand your centering. Many people report that after five or six months of centering, they develop a desire to center on the weekends.)

Centering is probably one of the most challenging practices ever to be encountered on the path to achieving our performance potential. It has been said that it is easier by far to stop a stampede of wild horses than to harness the wild stallion of the human mind. While no practice is more challenging however, the results are unequivocally equal to the investment, for when consciousness is transformed all life is transformed in equal measure.

One of the most beautiful stories in this context is a personal experience shared by one of our Academy members, Jeff. As a father of three, Jeff's commitment to The Academy was born out of wanting to be a better father. In monthly reports to his Academy peers, Jeff often shared some of the hurdles he was experiencing in this regard. The eldest child, 8-year-old Christopher, was becoming a real challenge. Found to be hyperactive, he often acted out both at school and at home.

Realizing that he couldn't expect Christopher to improve if he couldn't first improve himself. Jeff said he finally tired of his own rationalizations about his personal development. Up until that time he had been using his hectic schedule to justify his erratic centering program. Now however, feeling his responsibility as a father and role model for his son, Jeff decided that he would make his commitment to centering in two-week chunks instead of trying to do it all at once. He said that he felt that going for the "full cheese" (centering every day for the rest of his life) had pushed him too far and too fast out of his Comfort Zone. For his son's sake, Jeff made a firm resolve to center for two weeks and not to look any farther ahead than that.

He started his two-week program by rising at 5:30 a.m. and going into the living room to center. There in solitude and silence he would fulfill his daily commitment. A few days after he began this new regime Christopher happened into the room. At breakfast later that day Christopher asked his dad if he could get up early and "sit" with him.

Miracle of miracles, Christopher joined his father the next day. As Jeff instructed him in the way of centering, Christopher listened intently and then followed the directions. For two full weeks they centered together. A positive change in behavior was noted at Christopher's next teacher-parent conference. Jeff was pleased and astounded. He also found his son to be quieter and more peaceful than he had been all year. With these results, Jeff was easily able to recommit to another two weeks. Slowly, over time, he has turned his practice into a habit that has changed the texture of not only his life but also his family's.

PATIENT PRACTICE IS THE PROCESS

Although this is a glowing report most people experience a slow but subtle transformation. Therefore, we recommend that students let go of the need for immediate gratification. Results can best be achieved when we do not become attached to them. It is like planting and watering a seed; do your practice patiently and consistently with no thought of the result and the process will deliver outstanding rewards in due time.

Let me share another example with you. It is the story of two neighborhood friends, one a 5-year-old boy and the other, his 7-year-old neighbor. The older boy learned about vegetable gardening one day in school. That very day he came home and asked his mother if she would take him to the store to buy some seeds to plant a garden.

When the younger child saw his friend digging in his garden the next day, he asked him what he was doing. The older boy answered that he was planting a garden because he wanted to grow some carrots and cucumbers. The younger child immediately returned home and asked his mother to buy him some seeds to plant a garden.

The next day the 5-year-old planted his garden. He turned the soil, put the seeds into the dirt, covering them over and watering them just as he had seen his friend do earlier. Returning home from school the following day, the lad was so anxious to see the results of his work that he went out to his garden and dug up the seeds to see how they were doing. Every day he would do the same thing, run home from school and dig up the seeds. Meanwhile, his older friend was watering his seeds daily just as he had been taught to do in school. Several months later the 5-year-old couldn't understand why his neighbor had beautiful carrots and cucumbers and he had nothing but dried up seeds to show for his work.

The moral of the story is simple: don't be impatient with the process. Plant your seed by beginning the process and water it with a consistent dose of daily centering. Be still and do your daily practice without looking for a result and the results will follow in due time. Just as the child who plants the seed and waters it daily, trust that the daily process will pay off.

Remember that our lives are laboratories for learning. *The results that we seek will always show up as the mirror image of the investment that we make. Make the investment and the results will naturally follow.* Eventually, subtle differences will develop in your learning abilities as you begin to find yourself expanding to include the entire field of your awareness. You will find that not only is your receptivity enhanced but also your ability to access and retrieve information will be quickened. Over time, through this *inner work*, you will begin to experience differences in you mental acuity as well as in your ability to grasp new information.

Beyond this, we will only hint at the subtle differences that will be experienced in your sense of personal serenity and peace. All in all, centering is a general "healthing" technique. Just as it affects our mind and brain functioning, so it affects our emotional and physical responses in a positive way.

POWER POINTS

❀

Centering is to the achievement of our performance
potential as food is to our body.

❀

The mind is like a mighty ocean and thoughts are like
waves cresting on its surface. During normal
awareness we know only the surface waves;
thoughts splashing one upon another.
As we learn to center we begin to dive deep beneath
the surface cresting on our mental sea into
the depths of stillness where inner
knowing is encountered.

❀

The results that we seek will always show up
as the mirror image of the investment that we make.
Make the investment and the results
will naturally follow.

Chapter Seven

LEARNING AWARENESS STATES

"When the ancient wisdom, born out of
the stillness, begins to merge with the
ideas of a new generation, rather than
collide with it, a new society shall emerge
triumphant to resolve the challenges at
hand."

D. Trinidad Hunt

Our learning journey accelerates as we turn our attention
to the land of consciousness itself and the magic that is
experienced when perception is transformed. There is always a sense of elation when one breaks out of the boundaries of the box of their old thinking and enters an expanded
domain of awareness. The three states that we are about to
share are of this nature; they can be easily self-induced,
require very little practice to master, and deliver an expansion in awareness. We have shared them with thousands of
students who tell us that they have achieved seemingly
miraculous and almost instantaneous results with them. A
transformation of consciousness such as this is always an
exhilarating event, for a feeling of awe and wonder accom-

panies the ability to see with new eyes and to hear with new ears.

As for my personal experience, I have found that the more I played with the expansion of consciousness produced by the following three states, the more my learning improved and accelerated. What began as a simple practice eventually turned into a habit. Now I constantly depend upon the intuitive insights that accompany these states, whether in business meetings, personal conversations, or training sessions. I have found that my ability to listen and learn from any conversation or communication has perceptibly altered with the use of these states, for all of them have expanded my field of awareness.

Learning State #1: PFA

PFA - Present Field Awareness - is the first and most fundamental of the learning states in that it integrates inner and outer awareness. With PFA we expand our awareness to include the field of information that surrounds us. With PFA we release our sense of localized awareness and enter the field of consciousness itself. Done in conjunction with daily centering, PFA expands our awareness and learning, and helps induce the alpha brain wave state as we go about our daily business in the world. Ultimately, periods of hemispheric synch ensue, and herein lies part of its power.

Again, I discovered PFA out of my relationship with my grandfather. While he was extremely aware of the events in the world around him, if you were to look directly into grandfather's eyes you would instantly see a distinct difference in where his gaze was cast. Grandfather's blue-green eyes twinkled with an inner light and while he was totally cognizant of whatever he was engaged in at the moment, his gaze remained ever steady and focused inward. It was as if his attention rested on a deeply banked fire within yet paradoxically was all inclusive. Grandfather seemed to inhabit the space around him, for, as I said before, it hummed with vibrant energy.

Grandfather was by no means a hermit, nor was his life sedate in any way. In fact it was just the opposite. He was extremely active in the Honolulu community, hosting some of the world's great dignitaries in both the Buddhist and Christian faiths. He was a writer, a philosopher, a speaker and a teacher, and he worked an eight-hour-day until after his 90th birthday. The secret of his acute awareness was PFA.

PFA is developed through practice. To begin the practice, take a few moments to do the following exercise. Start in a sitting position in order to get a vivid experience of the feelings and awareness that this exercise induces. Now that you are centering daily, you need no more than one or two sitting practices before you can easily use the exercise whenever you are sitting, standing, or walking. What is important here is that PFA induces a state of heightened acuity and receptivity to the full field or environment around you and therefore enhances learning. Utilize it as often as possible and especially in any situation where you want to accelerate and optimize your learning.

PFA Exercise:

Close your eyes and withdraw your awareness by putting your attention on your breathing. Following the same word or phrase pattern that you are using in your daily centering exercise, inhale and exhale slowly, inducing the stillness. As you continue the practice for a few moments you will enter the deep centering silence and feel it penetrate both mind and body.

Continue to repeat your word or phrase as you again imagine the small vibrant orb of yellow-white light in the center of your chest. This time, feel the light of that orb radiating out through every cell in the center of the chest flooding it with warmth. Next, spread the warm light downward through the torso and legs igniting every cell with its energy. Then spread the light into the shoulders and down the arms into the hands; as you do, experience the pulsating energy filling every cell that the light enters.

Next, imagine the light rising into the neck, igniting the head and brain in full yellow-white radiance. Cleanse the entire system with light-energy for two to three minutes allowing the waves to wash out any toxins, tiredness or negativity found there. Complete the inner body work by amping up the light, turning your brain on to maximum capacity: awake, astute, brilliant.

Next, bring your attention to rest on your heart and extend your awareness outward from that area to a distance of about three to four feet around you. Visualize your awareness expanding as light all the way out to the walls of the room you occupy and even beyond, experiencing the room as if it were in you.

Notice the feeling of expanded awareness as you feel the entire environment flowing in, around and through you. Remain centered in your heart as you maintain this expanded consciousness for another two to three minutes. Then open your eyes, and walk around experiencing yourself as a *field of awareness*, having merged with the environment. Maintain this vibrantly aware yet peaceful feeling as long as you can. As it begins to subside continue with whatever you are doing. (Our audio cassette series includes PFA exercise.)

Periodically during the course of the day remember to remember to breathe, bring your attention to rest in the heart, and expand your awareness outward to experience yourself as an extended field. By making a game of it you will find yourself getting better at inducing extended periods of expansion as well as momentary flashes of heightened consciousness. In this state you will begin to experience rapid integration of information, extraordinary intuitive flashes and outstanding recall.

The more you play with this extended awareness, the more you will be able to instantly induce PFA and as you do so, learning will occur as if by osmosis. As every cell opens to experience the environment as itself and we experience ourselves as a field awareness and not a form with boundaries to it, the inner world and the outer world begins to merge and true intuitive knowing occurs. (See appendix for eye exercises to enhance sensory awareness and accelerate learning.)

Learning State #2: Whole Body Listening
The second learning state goes hand in hand with, and is an extension of, the first. It is a method of listening that turns hearing into a whole body experience and heightens both our receptivity and mental acuity. I discovered this learning awareness state about twenty-five years ago as a student of Yoga. However, for all practical purposes, I rediscovered it and began to utilize and understand it when I bumped into the Chinese symbol for the word "to listen."

This single, seemingly simple symbol contains a number of inner symbols; eyes, ears, heart and total attention. A dear Chinese friend once told me that total attention means to focus one's whole awareness. For the ancient Chinese, listening was an event that involved one's entire awareness. Finding that the Chinese concept of listening added powerful new dimensions to our limited Western concept of listening, I began testing it. I was ecstatic with the results, for I suddenly extended my perception of listening from a head experience to one of a head and heart nature.

Somewhere in this discovery process a totally miraculous shift occurred in consciousness. As I began to practice PFA in conjunction with extended listening, my entire body started to get involved in the listening process. It was as if other areas of my physical system could hear; every pore came alive with feeling and sensing. Perception expanded as I became aware of information that was beyond the realm of words or even body language. Intuitive whisperings and sensations entered my field of awareness; understanding and empathy deepened as I plummeted into a vast new domain of awareness regarding the person I was with.

At the same time, I found myself to be completely present

to every person. Up until that time, I had often drifted in and out while people were sharing with me. Naturally, I had learned the social grace of looking as if I was fully there, but in truth, I was often only partially there. Part of my attention would be with the speaker, while the other part was either preparing for what I was about to say or flitting to the future or past with things I needed to remember.

When I shared what I had learned with others, I found that mental wandering while listening was extremely common in our culture as well as others. No wonder communication and learning used to suffer; we weren't home! As I began training students in the practice of PFA and whole body listening, they reported similar experiences of heightened mental awareness. Again, they shared many instances in which their listening seemed to extend to the realm of the intuitive. All in all the consensus was twofold: enhanced communication both professionally and personally and more rapid integration of material being shared. By being taught to surrender their whole body to anyone who they were communicating with, they had each rediscovered the art of learning from listening.

Learning State #3: Groking

Grok is a funny little word that I discovered in my college reading. It came from a science fiction novel, *Stranger in a Strange Land*. Author Robert Heinlin coined the word to describe a very special type of communication in which each party understood the other completely. I have used the word ever since, for I have never found a dictionary definition that surpasses it.

To grok means "to get the essence of." To grok something is to grasp it; to get the marrow, the inner meaning, the crux, or the gist of it. To grok something is to understand both intellectually and emotionally, for it implies getting the feeling in your "gut," with your whole being.

If I ask you to grok something that I am about to tell you, I am asking you to get the essence of it. I am asking you to feel and understand it so deeply that you could immediately turn around and explain it to me, not by rote, but by translating it back to me in your own words. Groking is a natural function of the use of the two former learning states, and as such, is the essence of learning. To grok something is to internalize it so well that you have digested it, anchored it in your experience, and can then translate it back in your own way as if it were yours.

The results will speak for themselves as you practice these learning states. We are part of a universe that is a field of awareness, and the totality of that awareness is available to us for the asking. Expand your mind to include the entire field of consciousness around you with PFA. Begin to listen with every cell in your body and rapid, deep, long-term learning shall ensue.

You will find that just by having read about these states you will be easily able to induce them. Practice persistence. Make a past time of playing with these exercises as often as you remember to think of them and they will soon become habit. Be ready to discover a vastly expanded domain of awareness. As you flow out beyond the walls of the small self, and field and form merge, you will begin to embrace a continuity of consciousness that includes all things, events, and people within it.

POWER POINTS

❁

PFA blends inner and outer awareness heightening
insight and mental acuity. As every cell absorbs
its environment learning occurs as if by osmosis.

❁

Whole body listening combined with PFA seems
to awaken our intuitive abilities.

❁

Surrender your entire attention to the person who
you are with and you will rediscover the art
of learning from listening.

❁

To grok is to get the essence of...to grasp...to get the
marrow...the inner meaning or the gist of something
...to get it both intellectually and emotionally.

Chapter Eight

RECEIVING AND RETRIEVING INFORMATION

> "What an enormous amount of infor-
> mation we could call on if only we could
> gain access to this storehouse of forgot-
> ten knowledge we carry around in our
> heads."
>
> Michael Hutchison

While a computer has a limited storage capacity depending on the amount of memory we purchase, the normal
human brain has been perfectly constructed for infinite
storage and infinite retrieval. How often, however, have we
found ourselves hard-pressed to recall a piece of information or an incident? We can greatly improve our memory
proficiency by having a simple bit of information about
how the brain receives and retrieves information.

Information from our external environment is taken into
our internal memory bank (brain) via the doorway of the
senses. The eyes, ears, skin, nose and mouth are the main
doorways to the brain. However, we do not usually have a

sensory experience in a vacuum. At the same time as the sensory information is crossing the threshold of our awareness, we usually have thoughts about it as well as an emotional intuitive response to it. Put all of these bits together and we have a complete memory moment.

As the body receives these sensory, intuitive, emotional memory moment packets, it translates them into electrochemical impulses and stores them throughout the brain. In order to retrieve those images we need only think of part of the original image or sensation (an aspect of the sight, sound, smell, or emotion) and the entire image or thought can be easily retrieved.

Most of us have had personal examples of this experience. Have you ever heard an "oldie-but-goodie" on the radio and suddenly began to relive a teen-age crush? Have you ever passed a bakery and caught a special aroma that took you back to childhood? For me, certain smells after a heavy rain bring back rich memories of childhood scenes including the emotions of being a youngster. People from cold climates have shared similar experiences where winter smells bring back childhood memories.

To heighten memory recall we need only obey the basic laws of the unit with which we are working. In the case of our body suits, there are four simple programming guidelines that will help us improve our ability to retrieve information. They are: (1) The natural language of the brain is sensory-based. (2) The more senses we can involve in the learning process the easier memory retrieval becomes. (3) The brain responds to novelty, variety, change and associations and (4) for the learner, we can induce whole brain integrative learning by utilizing PFA in conjunction with the first three guidelines. All other guidelines are subsidiary and will be introduced later in the text.

101

As a facilitator or teacher seeking to induce a whole brain response to learning, use stories, symbols, diagrams, metaphors, music, and colors to stimulate the entire brain. These four guidelines create a single power point:

The natural language of our brain is sensory-based language, and the more senses as well as novelty, variety, change and associations that we can involve in the learning process the more we induce whole brain integrative learning.

In other words, we need to stimulate as many of the senses as possible in the learning process while we use change, variety and a multitude of associations to keep the mind alert and the entire brain awake to learning. Let's look at how we can apply this information.

The Role of Color in Learning

Color, color, color... no more flat black or blue on one page! The more colors we involve in the learning process the better. Whether you are a student, classroom teacher, or a professional trainer, the more color varieties you use, the more stimulation for the eye and brain. Also, the more you use colors in association with moods or feelings, the easier retrieval will be. An example of this would be using the color red to represent anger or the color blue to symbolize sadness.

We recommend that every personal learning journey begin with the purchase of a four-color pen available at most major variety stores in our nation. These four-color pens come in two styles: the basic blue, black, red, and green, and the new magenta, turquoise, orange and apple green. Many of the people we work with also keep an assortment of colored pens handy for brainstorming and planning. However, for basic business purposes as well as portability, we have found the simplest solution to be either one or two four-color pens. We will often refer to the use of these color pens in the next section of the book.

Naturally, the same rule applies for teachers or trainers. Use an assortment of colors when teaching. The key is to have five, six or seven colors available and to use at least two or three colors on one flip chart. This keeps the brain active and stimulates interest in the material. By doing so, it aids the student in staying alert to learning.

The Role of Sound in Learning

Once again the basic rules apply. As a learner in the training room, don't forget the power of the inner voice to validate and support learning. Mentally involve yourself in the training by answering the trainer's questions, intentionally and actively mentally engaging in the dialogue with him. This helps us internalize the teaching and make it our own.

As a teacher, remember that variety in pitch, pauses, tone, volume, and pacing serves to keep the mind alert and helps the learner stay with the material. Think of your voice as an instrument and utilize its full range during the course of any given training program.

The Role of Music in Learning

In this particular case, the music serves another and very special function in the role in learning. Specifically, Baroque music serves as a relaxant and heightens the entire body suit's receptivity to incoming information. We recommend that you have at least one of the tapes listed in the appendix on hand for use whenever you are studying, planning, goal setting or memorizing material. Beyond the Baroque, we have found that any quiet music which appeals to you will bring about relaxation and receptivity.

Pictures, Symbols and Diagrams

Think of it this way: Visuals of any kind trigger the right brain and stimulate a whole brain response to learning. For the student this means using symbols, pictures and diagrams wherever possible to represent the information as you are taking notes. You will see very clear examples of this

TOTAL MEMORY MOMENT

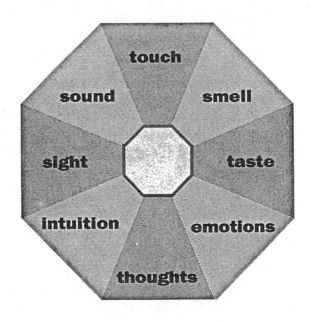

exhibited in the chapters on Mind Mapping and Power Notes.

Metaphors and Magic

All learning is enhanced by stories, allegories and metaphors. Whatever the means, the right hemisphere of the brain responds to any magical representation of the data or information being presented. In fact if you think about it, you will probably notice that what you remember from any meeting or training that you have attended is one or two stories that were told that day. Exceptional teachers and speakers are well aware that metaphors and stories will anchor in the long-term memory and will be more easily retrievable than data and information.

In short, stimulate, stimulate, stimulate! Keep the brain alive and alert to learning by using variety in color, sound and methodology. Activate the whole brain with symbolic references, pictures and metaphors. Finally, remember that sensory-based language is the natural language of the subconscious mind, and use it whenever you can to enhance learning and memory work.

POWER POINTS

❀

The human brain has seemingly infinite storage
and retrieval capabilities.

❀

The natural language of the brain is sensory-based.

❀

The more senses we involve in each memory moment
the easier retrieval becomes.

❀

The brain responds to novelty, variety and change.

❀

To stimulate whole brain learning use symbols,
pictures, music, color, stories and metaphors.

SECTION 2

POWER SKILLS
FOR THE 21st CENTURY

Chapter Nine

POWER SKILL #1: POWER NOTES

> "Memory is the cabinet of imagination, the treasury of reason, the registry of conscience, and the council chamber of thought."
>
> Saint Basil

In an age of information, powerful note-taking skills may become one of the most critical keys to retention and long-term memory. Although our brains are brilliantly constructed storage units, we often find that immediately after an event or a conversation is complete we are at a loss to access some of the specific information we need. Certain things may stand out in terms of importance to us, but because we didn't mentally highlight enough of the significant points much of it is lost deep within the recesses of the mind. Most often, it is never to be retrieved again.

Handouts are helpful in a training room but only to a point because they don't force us to use the powerful neural pathway to long-term memory that is established through the physical act of writing. Indeed, for those of us who want to master our ability to learn, power notes are crucial. It is a skill that not only allows easy retrieval of information later when it is needed, but it also assists in higher-order integration of that material with everything previously learned.

Power notes is a method of taking notes that utilizes the natural processing procedure of the brain. The note-taking system is based on the fact that the brain records all incoming sensory information in single-unit memory moments. In other words, intellectual information is never received in a vacuum. Along with the data being received are the sights, sounds, smells, tastes and feelings that are going on around and within the person receiving the information at the moment. These packets of sensory rich data are then sent to the various areas of the brain to be stored until we choose to recall them.

In order to retrieve the entire memory, we need only remember a small particle or aspect of the original whole. As we recall a part of the memory moment the entire memory is released into consciousness and we are able to relive the complete incident or recall the total piece of information.

Power Notes: Meetings, Training or Speeches

Power Notes are recorded on story boards. Story boards were originally used by Walt Disney to sketch out each one of his long-playing animated films. Every frame represents a single moment in the movie. When the frames are combined, movement occurs. Much like a movie, our lives unfold one still frame at a time. By recording our power notes frame by frame, we are later able to access an entire body of knowledge from a small amount of written data.

Using your four-color pen and any other writing implements you enjoy, take notes both in language and rudimentary pictures. Make your notes magical by using as many colorful and symbolic representations as you can. The critical key is learning to listen for the speaker's "power points."

Using whole body listening, listen with your total awareness, then grok the information and distill it down to its essence. As you have seen in the examples at the end of every chapter in this book, that essence is what we call power points.

Just as we learned while taking notes in school, each person's power points will be different. Yet each one's points will contain the heart of the information for that individual and will allow easy access to the entire memory of the teaching.

Capturing the Power Points

Prepare for all meetings, brain-storming sessions, or training programs by having story boards copied and ready to go. (See story board master in appendix for your use.) To capture the Power Points: (1) Induce PFA so that you are relaxed, present and focused prior to entering the learning situation; (2) Use whole body listening to grok the essence of the information being imparted; (3) Using your four-color pen, capture the power point on story boards; and (4) later, share the information with a friend or review it yourself using the story boards to trigger your memory. You'll be amazed at how much exact recall is available to you by means of this method.

Brain Shorthand

Actually, Power Notes started as a form of brain shorthand. Because I am always mentally working on solutions to professional challenges and because the human brain processes at lightning speed, I used to find myself losing many of the subtle Aha's that would surface in answer to my questions. The answers would rise like effervescent bubbles to the surface of my consciousness. But, because they seemed so simple, I would neglect to write them down, and they would quickly disappear never to return again. After awhile I found myself frustrated by the loss of potent information that would flit through my mind and then escape me.

Hence, the system of Power Notes was originally devised to capture my brain's own power points. As I started to record the quiet intimations that floated up from my inner awareness, I became extremely successful at retrieving solutions to problems and answers to questions that I had formulated earlier. It was as if I had made a miraculous connection with the vast storehouse of universal consciousness. The human brain is like a radio receiver; as we seek solutions to our life challenges, we send our RAS on a seek and search into the vast storehouse of universal mind. By sending my RAS on a seek and search, and then capturing the answers that my brain received (sometimes days later) I was suddenly catapulted into a whole new level of performance. Everything began working with ease and elegance, for I found no problem too big for the universe.

You will find that both the seeds to solutions you seek and creative opportunities for your future are revealed in the inner intimations and images that dance just beyond the shadowed veil of your awareness. You need only learn to take brain shorthand, for it is one of the easiest and most exciting creative methods in that it links us to higher-order consciousness. The subconscious is always waiting to help us; as we clarify the problem or the question we want answered, the subconscious immediately goes in search of the answer. Bit by bit its findings are released into our awareness. These inspirations and impressions only reveal themselves momentarily from behind the veil of awareness, therefore we must capture them before they slip away, back into the subterranean chambers from whence they came.

In order to do this I carry a time management binder with me wherever I go. Inside are monthly calendars and daily to do's, a four-color pen and a multitude of story boards for my brain shorthand notes. With the use of these tools and the willingness to actively take notes on my brain, I am always capturing fresh insight, new ideas, and creative breakthroughs that surface from the depths of my subconscious. Power Notes have truly been a key to my success as an educator, writer and public speaker.

The Genius Within

Just beyond the veil of our awareness lies the genius within. Like Michelangelo's David, this genius depends upon the sculptor for release from the stone. We are our own life artists; we chisel our destiny by the little things that we do daily and we mold our character by the habits that we form.

In order to make Power Notes and brain shorthand a part of the natural flow of our daily lives, we should take a moment to review the Comfort Zone. Every time we choose to change a habit, we run the risk of coming up against a bit of our own inertia or resistance. The natural proclivity of any living system is to maintain equilibrium or homeostasis.

Easy Info Retrieval
established through the physical act of writing it down

RETENTION · LONG-TERM MEMORY

INTEGRATE MATERIAL
with everything previously learned

Power Notes uses the Natural Processing Procedure of the brain.

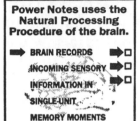

➡ BRAIN RECORDS ➡☐
INCOMING SENSORY ➡☐
INFORMATION IN ➡☐
SINGLE-UNIT
MEMORY MOMENTS

MAKE IT FUN!
colors & symbols
magical

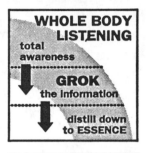

WHOLE BODY LISTENING
total awareness
GROK the information
distill down to ESSENCE

Capturing
relax
get present
focus
share with friend + review by self
use whole body listening to GROK info
use 4-color pen
Power Points

P R E P A R A T I O N

FOR:
• all meetings
• all sessions
• training programs

BY:
• having story-boards copied and ready to go

"BRAIN SHORTHAND"
human brain processes at LIGHTNING SPEED

take notes from universal mind

USE QUESTIONS TO CATCH AHA'S

even if answers seem simple write them down anyway

TIME MANAGEMENT SYSTEM GOES WHERE I GO
willingness to actively take notes
=
capturing fresh new ideas
creative breakthroughs

Like Michelangelo,

we must release our own David from the stone.

Every time we seek to make a change we are in fact asking ourselves to give up the safe plateau of comfort we have been inhabiting in order to stretch our boundaries once again. Naturally, this can be uncomfortable, but if we visualize the benefits of the new behavior, rather than focusing on the resistance, we can create the awareness and acceptance necessary to activate the change. Imagine being able to remember every critical piece of information that was exchanged during a business meeting or training program. Imagine being so self-sustaining and connected that there is no problem too big for you to solve, for all solutions come to you easily and elegantly. Imagine the raise you will earn when you are able to come up with solutions to certain company problems that no one has been able to solve. Wouldn't the discomfort of making the change be worth it if you could experience a drastic increase in your creative abilities?

This is the fundamental thesis of *Learning to Learn*. You are a great being living in a body suit that was built to support you in accomplishing your goals and fulfilling your life work. As long as your goals serve the good of the whole, you have the right to achieve them. The universal storehouse is unlimited, therefore our performance potential is unlimited. As we learn to tap into universal mind and capture the messages that it delivers through the connecting link of our brains, we discover that there are no creative challenges too big for us to handle. Using both the state-of-the-art tools and the processes and techniques included in this book, you will find yourself beginning to utilize the vast realms of knowledge available to each of us.

POWER POINTS

❀

Power Notes take the drudgery out
of note taking and makes it fun.

❀

Power Notes assist in easy memory access as
well as higher-order integration of material.

❀

Brain shorthand provides a miraculous connection
to the vast storehouse in the universal mind.

❀

Both the seeds to solutions we seek and creative
opportunities for the future are revealed
in our inner intimations and images.

❀

Learn to tap into the universal mind and capture the
messages it delivers through our brain, as we discover
that there are no creative challenges too big for us.

❀

We are our own life artists; we chisel our destiny by
the little things we do daily and we mold our
character by the habits that we form.

❀

Change your destiny one little habit at a time.

Chapter Ten

POWER SKILL #2:
RETRIEVING THE UNRETRIEVABLE
MEMORY FILE WITH THE MIND MAP

> "The very act of constructing a mind
> map is itself so effective in fixing ideas
> in memory that very often a whole map
> can be recalled without going back to it
> at all. A mind map is so strongly visual
> and uses so many of the natural func-
> tions of memory that frequently it can
> be simply read off in the 'mind's eye.'"
>
> Peter Russell

Have you ever had the experience of drawing a blank
when it came to preparing for a staff meeting, a group
presentation, or a talk you had to give? Being both a public
speaker and a teacher as well as an entrepreneur, I have
experienced this very situation on many occasions.

One particular incident comes to mind that seems to
exemplify the unretrievable memory file dilemma in a very
special way. It happened quite a few years ago when I was
asked by the American Society of Trainers and Developers

to give a speech at its Nevada conference. The chapter president called our office requesting a forty-five-minute talk on how to clear the resistance in a room when an audience had been required to attend a training.

This is a question that most trainers deal with on a regular basis, so it was not a new question to me. Thinking that I had much to say about the subject, I accepted the invitation to speak. However, when I sat down at my computer a few days later with the intention of quickly outlining my thoughts, my mind drew a blank. Old insecurities instantly flooded in, my stomach tightened, and my mind began to shut down. I found myself wondering what I could tell a group of trainers about clearing a room that they didn't already know. There I sat, feeling like a neophyte in my own professional arena. After fifteen years of public speaking and teaching, I felt as if I didn't know one thing about being in front of the room.

Then I recognized the reaction. It was the body's response to a perceived threat; the well known fight or flight adrenaline rush had taken over and I was totally in the soup! With ultimate determination I began calling on all the training I knew at that time. I started by giving myself a bit of affirmative self-talk to off set the powerful body response I was having. "I am not my body. I have been in this business for more than fifteen years and I do know something about it," I ascertained mentally.

As I continued to talk to myself with resolute determination, I suddenly realized the truth of what I was saying. I did have fifteen years in the industry and I did have some information on the subject of clearing a room stored somewhere inside of me. I knew that all I really needed was a way to retrieve the information. It was there but momentarily inaccessible. It was at that moment in this conversation that I was having with myself, that I remembered a technique that I had employed years earlier. It was a note-taking skill we had used in a summer training camp designed for Hawaii's teens. The technique was called mind-mapping and at that time we had used it more for the purpose of retaining information rather than retrieving it from long-term memory. However, as I considered the skill, it seemed to me that it would suit the job of memory retrieval just as well if not better.

Turning off my computer, I immediately cleared a section of my desk, got out a piece of paper and my four-color pen and began creating a mind map. Putting the topic, "clearing a room of resistance" in a circle in the center of the page, I began asking the following question. *"What do I know about clearing a training room of resistance?"*

Instantaneously, answers spewed forth from the depths of my inner consciousness. It was as if someone had opened the floodgates to my mind: ...I know it has to be done or people don't learn very quickly. I know that people come in loaded with expectations and that if the expectations don't match what's going on in the room they often shut down. I know that people who don't want to be in a training can often create a heavy energy in the room...

As my retrieval system slowed for a moment, I asked the question once again; *"What else do I know about clearing a training room?"* Instantly, I felt that well known pleasurable rush; the tension in my body released, and my mind began supercharging. My hand flew over the page and within the next ten minutes I had covered it with information on the subject.

In a short amount of time, I had regained a vast amount of information. As I looked at the page in front of me I was amazed at how much I really did know about clearing a

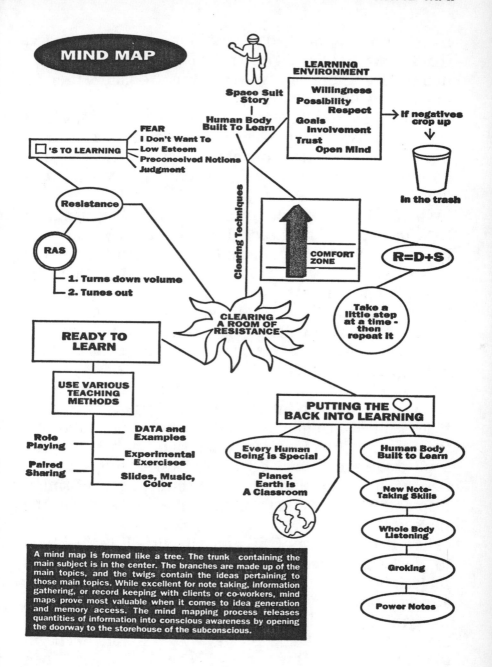

MIND MAP

LEARNING ENVIRONMENT

Space Suit Story

Human Body Built To Learn

Willingness
Possibility
Respect
Goals
Involvement
Trust
Open Mind

→ If negatives crop up

↓

In the trash

FEAR
I Don't Want To
Low Esteem
Preconceived Notions
Judgment

☐ 'S TO LEARNING

Resistance

Clearing Techniques

COMFORT ZONE

R=D+S

RAS

1. Turns down volume
2. Tunes out

CLEARING A ROOM OF RESISTANCE

Take a little step at a time - then repeat it

READY TO LEARN

USE VARIOUS TEACHING METHODS

PUTTING THE ♡ BACK INTO LEARNING

Role Playing

Paired Sharing

DATA and Examples

Experimental Exercises

Slides, Music, Color

Every Human Being is Special

Planet Earth is A Classroom

Human Body Built to Learn

New Note-Taking Skills

Whole Body Listening

Groking

Power Notes

A mind map is formed like a tree. The trunk containing the main subject is in the center. The branches are made up of the main topics, and the twigs contain the ideas pertaining to those main topics. While excellent for note taking, information gathering, or record keeping with clients or co-workers, mind maps prove most valuable when it comes to idea generation and memory access. The mind mapping process releases quantities of information into conscious awareness by opening the doorway to the storehouse of the subconscious.

room. In fact I now had so much material on the subject that I knew that I could never fit all of it into a forty-five-minute talk. The obvious next step was to organize the data into an intelligible whole.

That's where Power Notes came in handy again. First I prioritized the various sections on the mind map then made some critical decisions about what I felt needed to be covered in terms of the specific audience that I was addressing.

When I felt that I was pretty clear about the subject matter to be included in the speech, I took out a story board and began organizing the items in the order that I wanted to present them. Using my four-color pen, I color-coded the topics as I prioritized them into consecutive boxes on the sheet. Within a relatively short time I had the entire speech colorfully placed in story board format so that my eyes could follow the topic line by following the color changes as they moved down the sheet.

The speech received a standing ovation at the conference and generated much interest among the trainers. Beyond that, I learned an important lesson in the use of a mind map for memory retrieval. It is a lesson that I have constantly applied since that time. Whenever I am seeking information that has been long buried in my mind, I get out a mind map and begin by asking myself what I know about the subject.

The other advantage of this tool is that it will also help you to quickly and precisely locate blind spots on any given subject. By mind-mapping everything that I do know about a given subject, areas where I am lacking information begin to reveal themselves as the process unfolds. As I open a branch on a subject, and as I stay with the branch, I begin to pinpoint the spots where my knowledge is weak. Then

I know where to focus my research on the subject so that I can fill in the remaining areas I need to cover.

Further, I have found this to be an excellent management as well as writing tool. For managers it cuts mental preparation time for training sessions, staff meeting or sales presentations nearly in half. While in the area of writing, I have used it to lay out every book that I have ever written. The embryonic stage of any piece begins as a mind map on one sheet of paper and ends up as a full document some time later.

Beyond that, the tool is a powerful confidence enhancer and clarifier for by the time you have completed mind-mapping a subject, you definitely know your subject. Use it whenever you want to pull back any information from long-term memory for use at the present time.

POWER POINTS

❀

To retrieve the seemingly unretrievable
memory file use a mind map.

❀

In a short amount of time a mind map will help you
regain a vast amount of information.

❀

Use Power Notes to organize the material
that you brought back with the mind map.

Chapter Eleven

POWER SKILL #3: THE VISION PLAN

"A vision without a task is but a dream,
A task without a vision is drudgery, A
vision and a task is the hope of the
world."

Sussex England church 1730 A.D.

Vision Planning is one of the most powerful learning tools
I know. It creates the context for life change and gently
directs the course of both our personal and professional
transformation. Vision Planning maintains the structural
integrity of the body suit's natural learning ability and in so
doing, precisely directs our RAS in its seek-and-search for
our life's fulfillment.

Vision Planning establishes a bridge between this world
and the world of possibility by creating an inner blueprint
for change. It is man's sacred link to a world not yet
manifest, pregnant with potential and alive with awesome
promise. Through the Vision Plan we establish the possibility of achieving our performance potential by opening
our imagination and releasing the power of its creative

energy to form a sensory rich blueprint for the next stage in our lives.

It is easy and fun to create your own vision plan. In our work, we have directed thousands of professionals in the writing of both a personal and professional plan. Each person has reported that they have not only enjoyed the process but also that the end result changed their lives.

Having a vision plan lightens menial tasks, mobilizes and revitalizes our energies, and reframes our attitudes. It has the power to transform routine daily activities into magic by fueling the fire of our personal ganus. The function of the mind is to merge with what it focuses on. As you focus on your vision daily, you shall start to become one with it. Our personal potential for greatness is yet untapped. As we clarify our vision we move ourselves one step closer to the goal of becoming self-inspired, self-actualized humans.

Read the remainder of the chapter before you start the exercise. When you complete the chapter and are ready to stage the event, begin reading here as a review to set the space for the exercise.

Begin by imagining that you are staging a very special event, because, in fact, you are! Once the event begins, plan to have an hour and a half of uninterrupted time for the whole process. You will need the following:

SPACE:
Desk: with clean, clear, comfortable writing space
Lighting: comfortable and soft

TOOLS:
Writing paper: 5-6 sheets
Four-color pen, pencil or any writing tools you prefer

Tape deck or compact disc player
Music: accelerated learning music (See appendix)

EXERCISE:
When you are ready to begin the exercise. Turn the music on and sit at your desk. Close your eyes and enter the PFA state. When you are very relaxed and lucid ask yourself the following questions, *"If I could be whatever I wanted to be three years from now, what would my life look like? What do I see occurring? What kinds of things would I hear going on around me? How would I be feeling?"* Put yourself at the center of the vision by using the pronoun I, and then write your sensory rich vision as if you have already arrived in it.

Below is an example of a good vision format. However, once you begin, release the form and just let your inner awareness flow out onto the paper. If you hit a block in your writing, ask yourself, *"What else do I see? What else do I hear? What else do I feel as I experience my life three years from now?"*

SAMPLE VISION PLAN:
In my professional life I have become the vice president of Lowder Inc. I see myself sitting at my desk in the vice president's office. The sign on the open door has my name on it and just beyond the door in the outer office there is a feeling of friendly camaraderie exhibited in the office staff's conversation. It feels terrific to have achieved this new position, for I feel as if I earned it through loyalty, commitment and hard work.

At home I see myself with the family. The children are much older now. We are sitting around the fireplace talking together, and there is a definite warmth in the air between us. My partner and children are a total joy to me and I notice that the feelings that flow between us are very special.

I notice that my body feels firm, yet flexible. I can see myself running several miles every other day and spending an hour at the gym on alternate days.

I am finding it easy to maintain a low-carbohydrate, high-fiber diet. I can hear my inner voice congratulating me on my achievement. All in all, my body feels as if it is in a peak performance state. I feel mentally and physically healthy.

I have developed a consistent pattern of daily centering to enhance my mental development. I see myself sitting quietly on my bed in the morning before starting the day. As I view my body in the centering position I can see that it is lit up and humming with energy. I can feel my battery recharging as I prepare myself for a day at the office. The benefits of this practice have been phenomenal. I seem to be calmer and more peaceful than I've ever been while my mind is far more active, alert and creative. I feel great that I began this daily practice, for I know that it is one of the keys to my personal and professional effectiveness at this time.

You will notice the following guidelines were applied in the writing of the exercise above: *You are at the center of your vision. It is written in full paragraph form and in the natural language of the brain, which is sensory-based. It is also written in the present tense, as if you have already arrived at the end result that you seek.*

UPON COMPLETION OF THE EXERCISE:

Go back and change any future tense words to the present or past tense. For example; if you have written "I want to be"...Go back and cross out "want to be" and put in "I am." If you had, "I wish"...Go back and cross out "wish" and insert "I have."

If you find other areas that you left out of your vision such as travel, hobbies, spiritual development or educational advancement, add these at this time. You may also find that other sensory images come to you as you re-read your vision. Add these images at this time also.

When you feel totally satisfied with what you have written take a break. You have now completed the foundation piece for much of the work that is to follow.

This clearly defined Vision Plan will become the fuel for the fire of your action in the years to come. Therefore, copy it clearly or type it on a separate piece of paper and keep it with you in your time management binder. You should read it often and visualize the sights, sounds and feelings so that the experience merges with your inner awareness to form the blueprint for change.

When it has finally been accomplished and you have arrived at your intended destination, it is time to write another plan. This time you might try stretching a bit by writing a five or seven-year Vision Plan.

POWER NOTES

❀

Vision plans establish a bridge between this world
and the world of possibility. It is our sacred link
to a world not yet manifest, pregnant with
potential and alive with promise.

❀

Visioning creates the inner blueprint for change.

❀

A clearly defined vision plan becomes fuel
for the fire of action in the years ahead.

SECTION 3

BEHAVIORAL CHANGE SKILLS

Chapter Twelve

SELF-CULTIVATION AS
A LIFELONG PROCESS

"The end of education is character."

Sai Baba

Developmental psychologists tells us that in the final stage of human development we look back to view the totality of our life achievements. In his book *Childhood and Society*, Erik Erikson outlines the "eight stages of man," identifying the final stage as the period of "Integrity vs. Despair." This, he said, is a time for scrutiny and self-examination in which we measure the degree of our life's evolution, advancement and progress. Did we use our time or lose it? Here, in these latter years, we gauge the quality of our life experience and face the satisfactions as well as the regrets of the harvest.

One of the most valuable lessons that I ever learned in this regard came from my grandmother Gagi. During her twilight years I spent many hours in conversation with her about the meaning and purpose of life on Earth. Although her physical energy was beginning to ebb and her body was weakening, Gagi's inner fire still burned brightly. Somewhere in her 91st year, Gagi discovered that she had not completed one of her lifetime character goals. Her flame was suddenly rekindled for she realized that as long as she was alive she still had time to achieve her objective. With this exciting awakening her life blazed with the energy of her intention to complete this final goal.

From the moment of that discovery our visits became an opportunity for her to share her progress with me. She communicated every challenge and achievement, large and small. Even though she was in a wheelchair during those final years, her life took on the tone of a grand adventure for it was fueled by the inner fire of her goal. When my grandmother finally passed away at age 97, I knew by the transformation in her behavior, that she had accomplished her final mission.

To this day, the gifts that I received from that experience remain as some of the most enriching lessons in my life. I was in my late thirties at the time and the memory of those intimate visits stand out like high notes in a musical theme. They were notes that changed the entire musical score of my life. To this day I constantly reflect upon them to test the resonance and tone of my present life-tune.

Even though I was a bystander on the edge of the main event during that six-year-period, there were two outstanding realizations that I received from this exposure. Both of these realizations perceptibly altered my thinking and therefore my behavior. First of all, I came to view life as a process and to understand that that process was not complete until one's life was over. (Gagi died at 97 and her last six years were highly focused.) Secondly, I came to see that we, as human beings, can choose to change our behavior at any

131

point in that process. It is never too late to make a new decision. We are deciding beings, and as such, if we see that something isn't working in our lives, we can decide to alter it at any moment in our life experience.

Another realization dawned on me as a result of this chapter in my personal history. Gagi had changed my concept of aging. Until that time I had harbored an unconscious belief that when we retire we should be able to relax and let go, after all "we've earned it—we deserve to rest." This experience with my grandmother irrevocably altered that belief. I now viewed each stage of life, including the final stage, as a purposeful event. I realized that as long as we have life, we have an opportunity. Even as our body relentlessly proceeds in its aging process, we can continue to grow and develop, for learning is ongoing.

As a teacher, I reasoned that if other people had a similar model for aging early in their lives, it might change the nature of how they held life itself. Life could possibly be embraced as a sacred journey that unfolds in stages, with each stage delivering new opportunities for learning and growth.

Over time I integrated this experience and since then my teaching has been decidedly different; it is deeper and richer and resonates with the tone of lifelong learning. We now teach self-cultivation as the heart of that ongoing learning process, rather than a peripheral component of the process. In this regard, self-cultivation has become the main theme in our Academy as well as a central piece in our corporate training programs.

How Does it all Fit?

It may seem strange that such an intimate personal experience could so drastically influence our professional training and consultation work with businesses. But is that really the case? Let's take a closer look at historical aspects of what is occurring throughout the Western world.

As stated in the beginning of this book, a transformation is occurring in every nook and cranny of our planet; change is happening at the international, national, community, organizational and family level. From the family, to the church, to businesses to the community, groups of every kind are going through a revolutionary reformation both structurally and operationally. Although the specific changes may be different, the philosophical underpinnings of those changes whether at the national, community, business or family level are the same.

In other words, it is as if we have five different rivers, yet the water that feeds each of those rivers, along with all of their tributaries, is exactly the same. The basic tenets supporting this transformation are the principles of equality, inclusiveness, unity, and a commitment to a win-win philosophy. We are shifting our vantage point from that of the individual to that of the group, from "I" to "we."

The new paradigm, as we call it, embodies a whole new set of operating principles. Because of this, it demands new supporting behavioral skills. A metaphorical example of this concept of new skills that are necessary to sustain this new model, is the difference between the Lone Ranger approach of the past, and the Ninja-Turtle Team approach of today. As Lloyd Merritt Smigel notes in *Handle With Care: A Guide To Managing U.S. Employees in the 1990s*, "we are moving from the me generation to the we generation. We are entering an era where people want to contribute. People are becoming more aware, more participative, more caring." A new generation is being born and it is affecting every aspect of the organization.

ORGANIZATIONAL PARADIGM SHIFT

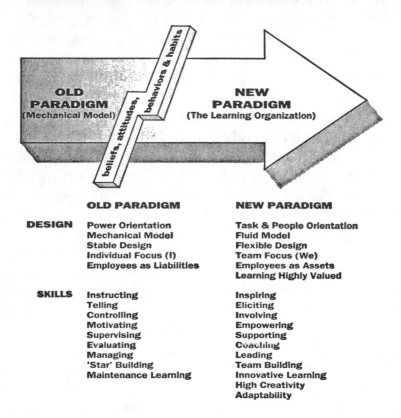

	OLD PARADIGM	NEW PARADIGM
DESIGN	Power Orientation	Task & People Orientation
	Mechanical Model	Fluid Model
	Stable Design	Flexible Design
	Individual Focus (I)	Team Focus (We)
	Employees as Liabilities	Employees as Assets
		Learning Highly Valued
SKILLS	Instructing	Inspiring
	Telling	Eliciting
	Controlling	Involving
	Motivating	Empowering
	Supervising	Supporting
	Evaluating	Coaching
	Managing	Leading
	'Star' Building	Team Building
	Maintenance Learning	Innovative Learning
		High Creativity
		Adaptability

The model above establishes the conceptual framework for the transformation that has been occurring in business over the last decade. This is a shift from the *industrial mechanical model* where the boss was in control to the *information age model* of the learning organization where everyone participates. Each of the tiny dots represents a single individual in the organization. Notice that each person moves through the barrier of their own attitudes and beliefs at a different time. Some individuals deeply steeped in the ways of the traditional model, take longer to adapt to the new ways. Others, not so deeply inculcated in the traditional methods, are able to move through their barriers more rapidly.

We are talking about the "human side of enterprise." At the organizational level, the entire staff must be educated in both behavioral and technical skills that promote and reinforce the new methods of human interaction in the new paradigm of the learning organization. At the family level, new skills and behaviors must be cultivated to ensure quality exchanges and interactions that produce healthy youth; citizens who will become contributing members of our nation.

In either case, skill development and behavioral development go hand in hand as the critical factors that ensure the success of this contextual shift. We cannot change a nation, an organization or a family without changing ourselves (or the selves who are the acting members of those groups). *In each case, behavioral and skill development is the goal while self-cultivation is a means of achieving that goal.*

Our company has guided this transformational process in dozens of organizations. Although each organization is unique, the basic underpinnings of change are the same. Transform the individuals and the business naturally transforms for a business is comprised of the individuals who participate in it.

POWER POINTS

❀

Self-cultivation is a lifelong learning model
for behavioral change.

❀

As human beings we can choose to change.

❀

Life is a process and as long as we're alive
we have an opportunity.

❀

Both behavioral and skill development are the
goals of change while self-cultivation is a
means of achieving these goals.

Chapter Thirteen

THE SELF-CULTIVATION LEARNING SYSTEM

"One of self-cultivation extends his awareness to know people and correct himself."

Ni Hua Chang

The original concept of self-cultivation is historically ancient; its roots can be found in almost every developed culture, including that of the ancient Hawaiians. However, the exact technology of change as indicated here, is now being supported by an ever-expanding body of scientific knowledge regarding how the human body suit learns.

What exactly is self-cultivation? *Self-cultivation is a lifelong learning method of behavioral change based on the metaphor of the seed in the soil.* While agricultural cultivation is about earthly gardening and deals with real seed and real soil, self-cultivation is about mental gardening and deals with new seed thoughts.

Both include choosing the new seed to be planted, then

tilling and turning the soil, fertilizing, furrowing, planting, watering, and finally harvesting. Both become the source of a new crop; one is the source of fruit and vegetables, while the other is the source of new behaviors and ways of being in the world. Ultimately the farmer in each of the fields will enjoy the harvest of his cultivation effort.

Notice the allegorical perfection of the self-cultivation model:

AGRICULTURAL CULTIVATION / SELF-CULTIVATION

Step 1: Choosing the new seed / Choosing the new qualities, characteristics and skills that you want to plant

Step 2: Tilling and turning the soil / Releasing past habits; being willing to change

Step 3: Fertilizing the soil / Creating the ganus or desire

Step 4: Furrowing / Writing and organizing seed-states (complete sensory rich blueprints for change)

Step 5: Planting / Planting new seed-state in fertile soil of the subconscious mind

Step 6: Watering / Daily focus on, and visualization of, the seed-state

Step 7: Harvesting the crop / Experiencing the new behaviors in your life

The ultimate result of all cultivation is that we reap the rewards of our work in the enjoyment of the harvest. For those who utilize the self-cultivation method, those rewards are experienced in new behaviors that lead to greater joy and satisfaction, enriching all areas of our lives.

Like agricultural cultivation, self-cultivation is an artful technology that greatly assists in achieving our performance potential. Through the self-cultivation method, we can develop the qualities, characteristics, and skills we want to express in the living of our lives. When we utilize it as a lifelong process, as my grandmother did, self-cultivation eventually leads to the refinement of character. In the final analysis, the nature of our character will determine the nature of our destiny.

POWER POINTS

❊

Self-cultivation is a lifelong process.

❊

Using self-cultivation we ultimately reap
the harvest of a well refined character.

❊

The nature of our character determines
the nature of our destiny.

Chapter Fourteen

CREATING YOUR OWN
SELF-FULFILLING PROPHECY

"One that desires to excel should endeavor in those things that are in themselves most excellent."

                                    Epictetus

Cultivation of any kind is an exacting science. If we plant a turnip, then a turnip is what we can expect to get! The same is true in self-cultivation. If we plant a specific behavior, we can expect to get that behavior in the harvest.

We don't ever expect to plant a turnip and get an apricot unless an apricot seed happened to get mixed into the turnip seed bag. So it is in self-cultivation, unless we happen to mix another behavior in the bag by accident, we expect to get what we plant. *Self-cultivation is a self-fulfilling prophecy*; therefore, it is vitally important to attend to the writing and clarification of the seed-states, prior to planting them in the soil of our minds. Because these seed-states will form the blueprint for coming changes, we must first carefully choose the seed, (step 1), then clarify those items in sensory rich terms (step 4) that the subconscious soil can easily receive.

The remainder of the chapter provides us with an opportunity to learn by doing. We will walk you through a step-by-step process. *It is advisable that you read through the chapter once to get an overview of the procedure so that you can then plan your event. Remember that our body suit learns by the use of vivid imagination. So once again, create a magical setting for yourself!*

EXERCISE FOR STEPS 1-4:

SPACE:
Desk: with clean, clear, comfortable writing space
Lighting: comfortable and soft

TOOLS:
Mind map model
Writing paper: 5-6 sheets
Six 3x5 note cards
Four-color pen or any writing tools you prefer
Pencil and eraser
Tape deck or compact disc player
Music: accelerated learning music

STEP 1: *Choosing the Seed (10-15 min.)*

The first step of the process is choosing the seed. To do this, we will utilize the basic mind-mapping tool shown in Chapter 11. Instead of using a flame in the center of the page however, we have placed a silhouette of a well-developed human being. That well developed being represents you.

This part of the exercise can be done right in the book or, if you prefer, the figure can be copied onto an 8 1/2 x 11 sheet of paper. By now, using your four-color-pen should be second nature to you, so title your page, "Five Year Plan" in one of the colors.

Now you are ready to begin this portion of the exercise. Again turn your music on, and sitting at your desk, or in a favorite spot of your choice, close your eyes, breathe slowly and evenly and enter the PFA state.

When you are feeling very relaxed and lucid, read your three-year vision plan to see what initially catches your eye; what qualities, characteristics, and skills immediately jump out at you. Then use this lead question to trigger the responses needed for this portion of the exercise: ***What qualities, characteristic and skills will I need to fulfill my three-year vision plan?*** Mind map your responses to this question as quickly as you can.

When you have completely answered this question and there is nothing else to add to your sheet, begin the next question. ***By the end of five years, what other qualities, characteristics and skills do I want to be exhibiting in my life?*** When answering this question let your mind roam over all areas of your life such as health, hobbies, skills, family, sports, exercise, professional advancement, educational, spiritual development and communication skills.

Again, mind map your responses to this question quickly.

If you hit a block and can't go any further, review the mind map on the opposite page and add any skills and qualities that feels right for you at this time.

When this portion of the exercise is complete, you will have the basic skeletal structure for transformation. The items you have in your mind map will form the basis for the direction of change that you will create in the coming five-year-period. Make a copy of this page for your time management system or keep it in a file at your desk, for you will need to refer to it every time you want to create a new seed-state (step 4) with which to work.

STEP 2 & 3: *Willingness and Ganus*

Now is the time to develop the willingness and the desire to achieve. Sometimes in our lives we may find that we *need* to do and what we *want* to do don't match. When this happens to me I use a simple three-step release formula so that I may continue to move through my blocks and barriers and proceed with my development.

I read these words to myself with my full heart and mind connected and with full faith in my ability as a human being to change my mind at any moment.

#1. **Remember to remember** who you are and why you are here. We are beings living in physical bodies that are on loan to us for the duration of our visit on the Earth. We are here on Earth to learn to be fine human beings. Our bodies were consigned to us to support us in achieving that purpose.

#2. **Remember to remember** that our Comfort Zone

may be safe, but it is not necessarily healthy. To be really healthy, we must be willing to get out of our Comfort Zones and grow, change and develop.

#3. **Remember to remember** the benefits you'll receive from developing the qualities, characteristics and skills that are on your paper. Then, if you need to, list those benefits.

By the time I finish going through the first two steps of my mental ritual I've usually released my resistance and am ready for step three. In this step I list the benefits that I will receive from developing the qualities, characteristics and skills that are on my mind map. Benefits always ignite the ganus, and ganus is the desire that nourishes the mental soil so that the seed can grow.

STEP 4: Organizing and Writing Your Seed-States (20-30 min.)

Let this next phase be a practice phase. In other words, give yourself permission to test and try, make mistakes and correct those mistakes, until your seed-state feels really good.

To do this, use a pencil on this portion of the exercise. Writing seed-states is a process, and as the process unfolds, we'll perfect the seed-states, and finally copy them onto a 3x5 card. These cards with seed-states written on them will become the blueprints for change as time goes on. Remember to take your time and enjoy the process for you are designing your destiny.

Choose one item from your Five Year Plan and write that item on the top of a clean sheet of paper. Ask yourself,

"What <u>exactly</u> is this item that I want about? What is my <u>specific</u> objective?" The key here is to capture the exact aspect of the item that you want to focus on. This aspect is your ultimate objective. The examples shown represent three different people who are focused on three different outcomes or objectives regarding patience.

EXAMPLES OF SPECIFIC OUTCOMES:

<u>Patience (1)</u>
I want to be patient with my 10-year-old when he is asking for help with his homework and I am feeling tired after a full and unnerving day at the office.

<u>Patience (2)</u>
I want to be patient with other drivers at rush hour on the freeway on the way home.

<u>Patience (3)</u>
I want to be patient when I am training Sally at the office. I want her to be successful at taking over the department and I know that will take patience during the orientation portion of the process.

After you have completed the first phase of the outcome clarification as shown in the example above, rewrite the statements taking them out of the future and placing them in present time. *In other words, write it as if you have already achieved it. Also, add the enriching details that will make it more vivid and real to your imagination.*

EXAMPLES IN PRESENT TENSE AND ENRICHED:

Patience (1)
I am warm and patient with Timmy as I help him with his math equations in the evening.

Patience (2)
I am completely relaxed and patient with other drivers during the evening traffic on the freeway.

Patience (3)
I am patient and gentle with Sally during her training process. She is responding remarkably well for she is learning the new procedure very quickly.

Now simply add the sensory rich aspects of the outcome you intend to achieve. *Ask yourself this, "What will I see when I am there? What will I hear my inner voice saying, or others saying to me when I get there? What will I feel when I get there?"*
Examples to elucidate some of the sensory rich details are underlined below.

EXAMPLES OF COMPLETED SEED-STATES:

Patience (1)
I am warm and patient with Timmy as I assist him in doing his math equations in the evening. I can see myself bending over his desk as I touch his shoulder gently to let him feel my quiet composure. I can hear the warmth in our voices

as we share our thoughts on a certain problem. I am totally <u>relaxed and energized</u> by the exchange, and <u>I can feel</u> that Timmy <u>is experiencing this same energy as it flows</u> between us. Homework has become a time for sharing and communication as well as learning.

<u>Patience (2)</u>
I am completely* patient with other drivers during the evening traffic on the freeway. I can <u>see</u> myself at the wheel on my way home from work. My body is completely <u>relaxed</u> and so am I, for I am <u>listening</u> to some soothing music that I picked up for this purpose. It <u>feels</u> really good to be using my drive time to relax and recharge my body and mind in preparation for an evening with the family. It <u>feels</u> great to be <u>at ease and in control</u> on the freeway!

<u>Patience (3)</u>
I am patient and gentle with Sally during her training process. She is responding remarkably well for she is learning the new procedure very quickly. I <u>see</u> myself standing beside her in the office. My <u>energy is calm and serene</u> as I explain the new filing system and I <u>see</u> her face light up as she <u>gets what I am saying</u>. The <u>warmth flowing between us</u> as we work together both amazes and pleases me. Our daily successes <u>show</u> that Sally is going to do really well as the department head of the future.

*Note the change in the first sentence; it didn't flow as it stood. Yours may change often before you create a satisfying version.

The test for whether or not a seed-state is complete is how you feel when you read it. Seed-states work like magic; they almost talk to you when they are right. When you read you seed-state and it feels like "YES!!", you've got it! Often you'll experience chills or, as the Hawaiians say, "chicken skin" when it is right on! When you finally get that YES response from your body and it feels really good, transfer the seed-state to a 3x5 card. This is your personal blueprint for change. Now we are ready to begin the planting and watering process. This seed state will become a focal point in your daily practice, for destiny is always done one single day at a time.

You may want to take a break before you begin the next section, or you may feel inspired to continue. Follow your feelings, for we have covered a lot of ground. Only you know your inner state, and either way, moving ahead or resting, will work for you!

POWER POINTS

❁

Self-cultivation is a self-fulfilling prophecy.

❁

Seed-states are sensory rich blueprints for change.

❁

Take time to design your destiny.

❁

Remember to remember who you are.

❁

Destiny is done one day at a time!

Chapter Fifteen

PLANTING AND HARVESTING

"The secret of success is constancy of purpose."

Benjamin Disraeli

In this chapter we will find the magical daily formula that leads to the success of your transforming venture. By following the simple procedure outlined here you will find the harvest to be very fruitful.

STEP 5: Planting the Seed (5 min.)
This step entails the strategic positioning of your seed-state in locations that you frequent on a daily basis. First copy your completed seed-state three or four times. You can do this either by copying it by hand onto three or four index cards or you can copy the seed-state on the copy machine and cut them into card size pieces. In either case, the next step is to tape them up in three or four locations where you spend most of your time during any given day. You might place one of them on your morning mirror, one on your night stand, one in your car and one on your desk at work. Then keep the original with you in your wallet or time management system.

By planting the seed-state in these various locations you create constant reminders of the new behavioral condition that you intend to achieve. Whenever you see the card take a moment to focus your attention on it by doing a quick inner imaging in which you create the feeling of reality about the new condition. Image it and you etch it into the subterranean chambers of the mind where the new etheric blueprint begins to replace past behavioral programming.

STEP 6: Daily Watering (3-7 min. daily)

In both the agricultural and mental fields, the growth of a seedling into a mature plant requires water. In this case, watering is a visualization process that is to be combined with daily centering.

At the completion of your normal centering session, when you are feeling very relaxed and focused, bring the vision of the seed-state that you have chosen before your mind's eye. See, hear and feel the new condition as if it were actually real.

Always enhance and intensify the image in the following two ways. First notice whether you are viewing the image of yourself at a distance. If you are viewing yourself at a distance, walk over (in your mind) and get into your own body so that you are seeing, hearing and feeling the vision from within your own body. Secondly, once you are in your body, imagine that you have the television-like ability to vivify and enhance the picture by turning up the color, volume and feelings. Imagine yourself amping up the inner sensory images until you feel completely immersed in, and at one with, the new condition. Make it so real that you merge with it completely.

Allow yourself to bask in the energy for as long as you want. Then, when you feel complete, have someone that you love or admire enter your mental scene and acknowledge you on a job well done. Hear and receive the good feelings that come with the acknowledgment. Finally, release the blueprint to the storehouse of the subconscious mind.

Remember that the function of the mind is to merge with what it focuses on. As you do your daily visualizing, the mind begins to merge with what it images, and behavior is slowly redirected toward the new.

STEP 7: Experiencing the Harvest

The harvest shall always be found in the field of our lives, for the value of this work speaks to us in the language of our own direct daily experience. As we patiently persevere in the cultivation process, we will begin to feel slight changes in the way we respond to the events in our lives.

If initiative is what you have chosen to work on, you will find yourself taking more initiative both on the job and in your personal life. If empathy was what you chose to focus on for the week, you will find yourself somehow being more understanding of others and responding to their feelings more.

Whatever the focus, little by little you will find your reactions changing, until one day you will notice that you have become what you at one time envisioned yourself to be. Like deja vu, you will have stepped into your own dream, except in this case our dream has been consciously created.

By beginning this practice, you have chosen to embark upon a very exciting journey of personal mastery. Self-cultivation is the secret of all extraordinary human beings down through the ages. In every culture, and in each generation, these outstanding humans have left a trail as well as landmarks for each consecutive generation to follow. As author Joseph Campbell says, "We need not embark on the adventure alone, we need only follow the thread of the heroes' tales that have gone before us."

And what is this tale? It is the life worth living, the life that is focused on the fulfillment of the unspoken promise of our birth. Every one of us is special and each one of us is specially endowed. Thus, the innate promise of birth is the promise to use the precious gift of life as well as the opportunity of time and the body we've been given, to develop our gifts and talents in service to all mankind while we are here. As we press out of our Comfort Zone and begin to actualize our latent capabilities, we align ourselves with life's pure purpose. Learning, expansion, and growth and service is what life is all about, and it naturally starts to feel good and right.

Ultimately, the result of this practice speaks for itself through the expression of our daily experience. Greater joy, satisfaction, and achievement becomes a self-motivating process. The more we experience the results, the more willing we become to take on the next level of expansion. Thus, having achieved a healthy crop in the first round, it becomes easier to do the preparing, planting, and watering in the next round.

Finally, the joy of the self-cultivation process lies not only in our own personal transformation, but also in the transformation of those around us. As our reactions change, so the reactions of those around us change. The result is a spiraling cycle of growth and expansion.

POWER POINTS

❀

Plant seed-states in strategic locations.

❀

Image the new state and etch it into the subterranean
chambers of the mind.

❀

The growth of the seedling is dependent upon
watering; in self-cultivation, daily watering
is daily imaging.

❀

See, hear and feel the new condition; make it so real
that you merge with it completely.

❀

Self-cultivation is the secret of every extraordinary
human being down through the ages.

❀

The harvest shall be found in the field of our lives.

❀

The life worth living is a life that fulfulls the unspoken
promise of our birth.

Chapter Sixteen

MODELING
The Fast Track To Mastery

*"People seldom improve when they have no
other model but themselves to copy after."*

Oliver Goldsmith

One of the gifts of being a trainer, is that I have the opportunity to engage with hundreds of people during any given month. The side benefit of this is that I continually encounter a variety of viewpoints and perspectives.

Every human being views the world through a different lens and each has a different set of life circumstances and stories to share. As a result, I have a constant opportunity to adjust and expand my outlook.

Every person is my teacher, what they have learned through their experience, I can absorb by listening. In this way, I have consciously accelerated my learning time by vicariously gaining from the experience of others.

MODELING IS MERGING

Naturally, this ability is not confined to the domain of trainers. It has been said that every great human being stands on the shoulders of another great human being. History abounds with the names of those whose youth was absorbed in a passionate love of earlier models; General George Patton, John F. Kennedy, Martin Luther King, Amelia Earhart are just a few from the list of hundreds.

We need not reinvent the wheel, rather just observe or study those around us or those who came before us, who exemplified the attributes that we ourselves want to attain. Modeling is a master key to success because it utilizes the three mental keys of attention, imagination and focus. Modeling is the fast track to mastery because it is the ability to instantly imagine or "put on" the attributes of another. We can all accelerate our learning time by assimilating the lessons of others in our environment, and modeling is one of the finest methods that I know of to do this.

Some time ago I was having a discussion with Art, a friend of mine in the industry, and the conversation somehow turned to the subject of modeling as a learning mode. As our talk progressed he began to share the story of his success which elucidates this concept powerfully.

Art said that he spontaneously discovered modeling in the process of life itself. As a teen frequenting Waikiki he used to wonder what made the surfers so popular with the young female mainland tourists. In the beginning he didn't understand it; they weren't so special in their looks nor their physique, so what was their secret? As Art began to observe the surfers more closely, he discovered that they seemed to have one quality in common. They all seemed to have a relaxed confidence in their exchanges with others. Their calm manner and quiet assurance lent to the magnetic feeling of self-reliance that surrounded them. Art decided he wanted what they had and began copying their mannerisms and body language. It worked like a charm and you can guess the results that occurred.

Some time later, when Art entered college, he found that the grades he wanted to achieve somehow always escaped him. Although he put in the study time, he found that when the testing period rolled around, his grades weren't equivalent to his investment in his studies.

One day, completely frustrated by the results and wanting to do better, Art found himself in another testing situation daydreaming of succeeding. His daydream took a very specific form however, in that he found himself pretending to be the teacher. Art's thought process went something like this:

"This is ridiculous, I've studied for this test! It would be different if I hadn't studied but I'm tired of getting C's when I study the material. If I were the professor I would know every answer to every question in front of me. I'm sick of getting low grades so I'm going to pretend to be the teacher and take my own test."

Fully enraptured by the daydream, Art had mentally shifted from feeling as if he were the one being tested to the one who was giving the test. He had shifted from a victim role to a creative role, from having it done to him, to being the doer. It was a drastic role reversal and from that moment on, Art's body completely relaxed.

After all, why sweat the small stuff; he was now the teacher doing the test that he had written himself. It suddenly felt as if none of the test was foreign to him; he glided through the questions, experiencing each one of them as if they were his own. Answers came to him with ease.

It was a math test, and numerical equations popped into his head. Art sailed through the entire final, completing the test in record time. He handed his sheet in before anyone else was finished and left that day feeling relaxed and completely at ease.

When the math scores came back days later, Art received a paper with only two items wrong out of one hundred. It was the highest score in the class and one of the highest scores that Art ever received in his college career. He said that the results of this fantasy flight were so miraculous that he frightened himself and he dared not attempt it again. It was only years later that Art discovered that he had bumped into one of the great secrets of success; *what we model, we become!*

ACT AS IF.....

Modeling is an excellent method for assimilating specific attributes, but what if there aren't any behavioral models available? At such times we recommend the "act as if" frame. The "act as if" frame utilizes creative imagination and the potent power of our mind's resourcefulness. *Act as if you were...whatever you wanted to be.*

The secret to utilizing the vast creative ability of the subconscious, is to ask it questions. As we saw in mind-mapping, our mind can't resist questions; it automatically responds.

Let's say that you have discovered that you are totally impatient while standing in line at the grocery store or in the bank. You know you *should* be patient, but your body goes into automatic and the adrenaline flow begins whenever you're standing in a line for more than a few minutes.

Further, all of the models you were raised with exhibited stress signals when they had to wait for anything. Where do you go to learn a new behavior if you don't have any models in your experience? The answer is simple; you go to the greatest creative generator of all times, your own subconscious mind!

Begin by asking yourself how a patient person would act while standing in line waiting for groceries. How would a patient person behave? How would a patient person feel while standing in line? What would the voice in a patient person's head be saying? What would a patient person be doing while they were waiting in line? Where would a patient person put his/her attention while waiting in line? How would a patient person's body feel? What would a patient person's physical mannerisms look like as he/she waited in line?

Our mind is extremely inventive, it loves to generate anything! So you might as well have it generate something positive! When we play the "act as if" game, we channel our mind's energy in a constructive way into the creation of new and more appropriate behavioral options. No matter what your role in life, whether a mother or a manager, use the "act as if" game to develop any attributes or skills that you desire. To play the game you simply ask yourself a set of simple questions and let your natural creative imagination do the rest:

How would a person who was_____ act?
How would they behave?
How would they feel?
Exactly what would they be doing when engaged in this activity?

Then, to accelerate the assimilation process, combine the "act as if" game with visual imagery. When you find yourself alone for a moment, enter the PFA state and visualize yourself being exactly what you want to be. Run a number of different scenarios in which you see, hear and feel yourself practicing the attribute or skill you're working on. Finally, during the day remember to remember to act as if you are what you wanted to be.

MENTORING

Mentoring is a gift that comes to us from the outstanding achievers of the past, for mentoring *was* the ancient path to mastery. The dictionary defines a mentor as a "great counselor, guide or teacher." The word comes from the name of a man who lived and worked with Ulysses. Legend has it that when Ulysses went out to conquer the world, Mentor stayed home to take care of Ulysses' son and his properties. When Ulysses returned after eleven years at sea, Mentor greeted him at the gate, an enlightened man. While Ulysses had conquered the worlds abroad, Mentor had conquered the worlds within and his name became synonymous with "great teacher."

Modeling and mentoring are very different in that modeling usually assists in the acquisition of an isolated quality or attribute, while mentoring is the study done under an exceptional trainer for the purpose of mastering an art or a skill.

Mentoring is the finding of, and committing to, a master teacher. It is one of the quickest paths to mastery, for it is the choice of following the straighter line rather than the meandering trail. In every ancient tradition, whether it be the martial arts schools of the East, the hula halaus of the Pacific, or the artist guilds of the Renaissance, mentoring was *the* method of mastery for the serious student.

Today, mentoring may be seem to be relegated to the hallowed halls of the Martial Arts Dojos, the drama schools of New York City or the fine arts schools of the East Coast and Europe. However, there are great and even extraordinary teachers available for study in almost every area if you are only willing to seek them out.

SELECTING A MENTOR

Mentoring has long been out of favor in the Western culture where quick-fix methods have often superseded long-term mastery. Today however, more and more people are recognizing the need to enter the realm of mastery where the chiseling and refining of character is an inherent part of the long-term learning process. If you happen to be one of these people, it is important to realize the value of a good mentor; long-term learning with mastery as its goal is accelerated under the guiding hand and eye of a master.

Often a mentor appears by readiness and not by conscious choice. There is an old adage in the East that says "when the student is ready the teacher appears." When this is the case, be both thankful and willing, for the universe has deemed you ready and provided you with a way to mastery. To be given a great teacher, is to be given a great gift, for the true sign of greatness in a teacher lies in the triumph of his students.

In seeking a mentor, you will find that the mentor:
#1 Is seen in his Students
The art of a great teacher is practiced on the canvas of

his or her students' lives. Therefore, one way we can come to know if we have found a great teacher is by the performance of that teacher's students. Observe the student for he or she is the extension of the teacher.

#2 Models and Honors his Art
Mentors teach best by example and the example that they set is their love for learning. It doesn't seem to matter whether the mentor's enthusiasm or his art is expressed quietly or passionately, it is definitely there. The great teacher has come to greatness through a love for the art that he practices.

#3 Exhibits High Esteem
An exceptional teacher demonstrates a quality of high regard for the students that he teaches. Having earned his status by confronting the worst and then choosing the best in himself, he knows that the path to freedom is a long and arduous one. He openly respects the warrior, for he knows well the hills and valleys to be traveled in the sacred journey of mastery.

#4 Changes Meanings
A mentor reverses meanings in the mirror of life. Like Alice in the looking glass, when we enter the path of mastery, we enter an upside down world, where pain means gain and plateaus mean that we're on the way to the goal. The mentor is the creator of context, a trailblazer and a guide who can help us gain an understanding of the rules in this new domain. Having traveled the road before us, he can provide an invaluable map of the territory. By defining the terrain, he can assist the student in recognizing the

signposts and signals of learning and growth along the way.

Those who follow the path of mastery soon discover that learning never happens in a vacuum, and that what they learn in one area generalizes and spills over into other areas of their lives. Attributes such as discipline, commitment, patience, persistence and ganus are developed on the path to mastery no matter what the art or skill. Ultimately, as we develop these attributes in order to achieve a goal in one area, we find that they are then available to serve us in all other areas of our lives.

A Personal Awakening

By embracing models and mentors and by emulating those who personify what we seek, we quicken our progress. For a long time, I sensed that love was the key to this process, but I didn't know why. In my own personal journey, my grandparents were my mentors. From my grandmother I absorbed a love of language; my passion for poetry, speech and writing came from her. From my grandfather I learned to cultivate the remarkable attributes of greatness that his life exemplified. Following in his footsteps, I made centering a daily practice and discovered discipline to be the key to my personal freedom.

As *Starwars'* Luke Skywalker realized, death cannot separate us from our mentors. And so it was in my case, through centering, focus, and vivid imaging my relationship with both grandparents was maintained long after each one had left this life. Questions such as, "How would Gagi have approached this piece of writing?" or "What would grandfather have done in this situation?" or "If grandfather were here, how would he answer this question?" consistently triggered spontaneous solutions to the every day challenges in my life long after they were gone.

Through my love and open adoration for my grandparents and through vividly imagining their thinking, I began to feel as if I were merging their consciousness with mine. Thus it is that the bond of love cannot be severed. In the journey of mastery, two souls are sealed; student and mentor merge as one. The death of each grandparent brought with it a merging of minds that crossed the void and rent the veil of separation. This culminated in one of the most important discoveries of my life for I had bumped into what I consider to be one of the most powerful planetary laws of learning that there is.

The function of the mind is to merge with what it focuses on. It is because of this law that whole body listening and PFA allow us to merge with others and our environment. It is because of this law that self-cultivation and modeling work and it is also because of this that children, like sponges, absorb the qualities and characteristics of those they love. It is also the reason why teachers play such a critical role in the life of our children and why teaching may be one of the most important jobs in our society; outside of the parents, the teacher has more contact time with our children than almost anyone else. The teacher's role as a behavioral model and mentor cannot be underestimated.

In this ancient secret of secrets may also lie the hope of the future, for it is because of this law that we can make quantum leaps in our learning and development. This means that as a species we are capable of revitalizing the planet in a single generation if we so choose. At this critical juncture in our history, let us utilize this law in the healing of our planet. By concentrating our focus and the light of our attention and imagination on the great beings in our planetary history, we can begin to merge with the high values they exemplified.

It is for this very purpose that the great ones came. Moses, Christ, Mohammed, Buddha and many more were sent as models of perfection and grace to lead mankind out of the wilderness of lowly experience. They continue in their mission to this day, for as we honor our teachers and utilize our minds to merge with them, we accelerate the absorption of their fine attributes. Finally, as more and more of us become engaged in this high endeavor, we will move rapidly toward the critical mass needed to transform our planet.

POWER POINTS

❁

Every great human being stands on the shoulders
of another great human being.

❁

What we model we become.

❁

Play the "act as if" game; act as if you are whatever
you want to be.

❁

Questions are the key to generating solutions.

❁

The function of the mind is to merge with
what it focuses on.

Chapter Seventeen

SLEEP AS OUR ALLY

"To sleep, perchance to dream."

William Shakespeare

If I could sing of the life perfected and of performance potential achieved, my song would surely have to include the natural rhythms of daily consciousness. We would then introduce into the composition a harmonic blend of trust in and appreciation for our relationship with all life and with life's process.

Trust in and appreciation for our connectedness are central themes without which we become separated from our own sacred journey, feeling ourselves to be, as Robert Heinlin said, "strangers in a strange land." With trust, appreciation and connectedness restored, we find ourselves bound on an exciting adventure in consciousness in which each aspect of our lives whispers of our own awakening and self-discovery.

The change in daily rhythms, the cadence and cycles of

night and day, can then be honored and utilized for the gifts that they confer.

SLEEP AS THE PROBLEM SOLVER

Let us begin to explore the phenomenal power of sleep to deliver solutions to daily problems. Sleep is the doorway to deeper awareness for when the gates to the hidden chambers of the mind are unlocked, the creative genius of the universe comes to life within us.

My discoveries regarding the power of sleep began in my mid-twenties. During that phase of my life I was spending a lot of time doing dream work. I kept a pencil and a notebook by my bed and in the morning I would write down everything that I had dreamed from the night before. Over time my dream world became potently alive with precognitive visions. I found myself dreaming of experiences and encountering people and events before they happened.

As time went on my dreams became so profuse that I was filling pages with my dream material. Life was becoming a deja vu experience in which I would recognize the days' events as they were unfolding. Eventually work began to take more and more attention, and as my life got busier I found that I couldn't keep up with the extensive daily entries that I was making. In time my morning journal began to get sketchy as I subordinated my dream work to "real" work and the "real" world.

It was then that I discovered that one need not remember all dreams to benefit from the tremendous problem solving power of the subconscious. I was teaching school at the time and the rigorous schedule that I was keeping precluded any extensive personal work beyond the normal self-cultivation process which had become part of my daily routine. I found that I had reached an impasse with the group of thirty, fifth graders that I was teaching. Although everything looked OK on the surface, there was a general complacency in the group that disturbed me.

One evening I went home more than mildly disturbed by the general lack of inspiration and enthusiasm that I was experiencing from the students. On the whole they hadn't discovered a passion for learning, and as a result, I was still pulling, pushing, and prodding to keep them moving ahead. I was especially distressed as I retired that night. Feeling myself to be a failure, I intensely turned within asking over and over, "What is missing? What is it that keeps them from getting 'turned on' by the learning process?" I went to bed totally stumped, and after tossing and turning, I finally fell into an agitated sleep.

The next morning I awoke with a crystal clear answer to the question. "The children are not involved in their own learning process. They're uninspired because they lack involvement." The answer was so clear that I felt as if I was in the middle of a conversation, so I continued with the logical next question, "So what do I do to get them involved?" The answer burst up from inner regions of awareness not consciously known by me: "Teach them goal setting!"

"Teach them goal setting?" I queried. And the answer bubbled up again. "Guide them to set some educational goals and goal setting will involve them in the process. It makes the learning process their process instead of yours."

I went to school elated that day, anticipating the ease with which I would set things straight. After all, I was given the word! I thought that all I had to do was carry it out; so I was bound and determined to start into the new regime immediately. My first day at "the new way" proved to be a complete disaster, for as I started to teach goal setting the children went into complete confusion. Upon reflecting that evening, I realized I had not even considered *how* I was going to teach goal setting. This was a class of fifth graders, not adults; in my excitement, I had failed to consider that my presentation needed to be adjusted to the age level. I had completely overlooked phasing the goals in order to allow the students to experience their success in short stages.

Back to the drawing board. That night I asked the critical question, "HOW? How am I to set up this goal-setting procedure as part of an ongoing process and not in an instant fix manner?"

This time, the results of my dream-time were different. I did not get an immediate answer as I had the night before. Instead, the answer came to me slowly over the period of the next week as I did the planning that I knew I needed to do.

The process had to be well thought out, and as I sat with pencil and paper before me, the plan slowly unraveled. Each evening, before going to bed, I would review the work of the day and ask for more information to be revealed.

The process worked like a charm! Whenever I bumped into a barrier, I spent a moment before going to bed, consciously thinking about the problem and asking my subconscious for help with the solution.

I was so successful with the students during the course of that year that the results caught the principal's attention, and she asked if I would be willing to teach what I had learned to all of the fourth, fifth and sixth grade classes. Naturally I accepted, and the next few years proved to be the most exciting in my school career. In addition, I trained the faculty in those respective grade levels.

SLEEP AS THE BARRIER BREAKER

Quite by accident, I discovered years later that I could use this same method with my writing. By that time I had become quite at ease with "talking to myself" but what I didn't know was that I could generalize what I had learned, using it in other areas. In other words, I had confined the process to helping me gain solutions to daily problems but I had not fully allowed myself to trust it in all areas of my life.

It happened during the period in which I was writing my first book; it was then that I discovered a new relationship with that dreaded phenomena known as writer's block. As one day of writing unfolded into the next I began to observe that my writing rhythms had shifted from rigidity to flexibility. I had unconsciously begun to accept the hills and valleys of creativity. Every time I hit a barrier, block or turning point in the writing, rather than fight it, I would go for a walk, or take a popcorn or hot chocolate break. In other words, rather than confront the block directly, I would skirt it. I would deliberately change the subject.

Then, one day I hit a wall! It felt as if it was as wide as a mountain and as high as the sky. I wrestled with it, fought with it and lost to it. The day became a bleak torment and my mind felt as if it was cast into darkness and the book would never be finished. That night I fell asleep exhausted; I had entered the arena and battered myself against the barrier all day and I was deeply tired.

The next morning, wonder of wonders, the answers unfolded during my centering process. They unraveled easily, as if someone or something had gone into the mental mechanical workings that had been jammed the day before, and disengaged them.

I immediately went to the computer and began typing. As my hands flew over the key board and the story poured out, I realized that I had just encountered a major lesson in creativity and in life. *Trust life and life's processes because life works!!* The next time I hit a major barrier, I tested it to make sure that I couldn't get around or through it and then I took the rest of the day off and played. That night I took a moment to focus my mind on having my writing flow smoothly the next day, and I went to sleep. That morning I went back to my computer to find that play and the sleep of the night before had fulfilled its promise. I wrote freely all day and fell asleep tired that night, not from a battle, but from a breakthrough!

SLEEP AS LEARNING'S ALLY

During The Academy, training members arrive on Friday evening to spend the weekend at the learning center. On Saturday students go through a full day covering everything from discussions on the purpose and meaning of life, to art, dictionary study, body work and dance. We then tell them to go to bed, and let sleep take its course, for sleep is learning's ally. *Sleep is to learning as digesting is to a good meal;* it is the great synthesizer accelerating the assimilation of our daily experience and lessons.

In sleep's kingdom, conscious thought is exchanged for symbolic languaging and a metaphorical referencing system replaces logic. When we enter the realm of sleep we enter the territory of natural knowing in which the activities and events of our daily experience are brought before the subconscious for examination. It is here, in the inner regions of the human mind, that the instinctive sorting and sifting mechanism is freed from the grip of conscious awareness and everything learned from the day before is combined with all previous experience to form a new integral whole.

Sleep is the great integrator; it allows the subconscious an opportunity to synthesize our learning from life events, conversations, and experiences. To this day I use sleep to solve problems or to develop a speech or training material for a workshop. As a teacher, I have also come to support my students in trusting sleep and utilizing the gifts that sleep confers. Rather than struggle with learning, we teach students to let the rhythms of sleep assist and support them in the integration process.

POWER POINTS

❀

Sleep is the doorway to deeper awareness; let the
creative genuis of the universe help you achieve
solutions for your life.

❀

Trust life and life's processes because life works!

❀

Sleep is to learning as digesting is to a good meal;
is it the great assimilator of our daily
experience and lessons.

❀

Sleep is learning's ally.

Chapter Eighteen

FOCUS FORWARD TO THE FUTURE

"You see things and you say Why;
but I dream things that never were
and I say Why not?"

George Bernard Shaw

In the world of possibility where life works, all things work to our advantage and so it is with the Comfort Zone! The more basics that we can consign to the domain of habit, the more we are able to focus on the bigger picture of our lives. By consciously expanding our Comfort Zone and filling it with healthy habits, we free ourselves to take on larger goals and more challenging projects.

Good habits are a great advantage! What would life be like if we got out of bed every day..... or we didn't.... then we went to the basin to brush our teeth... or we didn't. If everything we did every day depended upon our moods, we'd be in deep "kim-chee" (as the Hawaiian island saying goes). A child of four may or may not brush his teeth every day and we are patient with that child's learning process. However, a 40-year-old who hasn't made brushing part of his daily ritual is found to be socially unacceptable.

Habits are wonderful, without them we would never have time for any higher-order thinking. Through the conscious acquisition of healthy habits, we are able to free the potent power of our attention to concentrate on higher-order thoughts, plans, and challenges. As we creatively expand our Comfort Zone, with each new and healthy habit that we add, we free more and more of our attention and energy for other things.

The discovery of the benefits of healthy habits is probably one of the most exciting aspects of The Academy training. By studying the attributes of greatness and by the use of a tool that we call "tracking," Academy members learn to view their lives through the lens of single aspects of greatness. The effect is very much like putting a tinted lens on a camera for a period of time to see how life appears when viewed through that particular shade or tint.

Like a scientist in the laboratory of their lives, each student is asked to observe themselves and their behavior through the lens of patience, for example. What they discover during this viewing period is the nature of their present relationship with the word. They are then asked to track the results of their observations. As a student begins to study his tracking notes, he discovers both strengths and weaknesses in relationship to the attribute and he is then able to highlight specific focal points for improvement.

The fundamental law that determines the results elicited through this method is the law of unconsciousness: *That which is unconscious runs our behavior.* In other words, tracking reveals unconscious inner patterns that are driving our external behavior. As the process unfolds, students are able to make clear distinctions about which behaviors serve them in awakening their full performance potential and which do not. As self-awareness expands and students find themselves choosing new and healthier habits, they begin to experience higher levels of competency, personal satisfaction and improved quality of life. The undeniable outcome of all this has proven to be a heightened sense of responsibility and accountability for one's personal and family life as well as an expansion of service to mankind via contribution at the organizational and community level.

One of our Academy graduates, Lovell Harris, made a special point of thanking us for this principle of healthy habits. A year after completing The Academy he was voted the number one drug and alcohol abuse counselor in the United States Navy. He received a Medal of Honor in Washington and I had an opportunity to talk with him a few months later. He said that the number one key to all of his achievements was the development of healthy habits. "Things have changed so much for me, Trin," he said. "It used to be that when I had a bad day I had a bad day! Now, when I'm having a bad day the healthy habits I've developed kick in and carry me through the day anyway. No matter what, I get the job done regardless of my inner weather forecast!" He added, "If I could share anything with others it would be this; create healthy habits, and healthy habits will carry you when you need them!"

DESTINY IS DONE ONE DAY AT A TIME

The message is clear; destiny is transformed one day at a time. Rehearse, prepare, practice and perfect for we are living but a short time upon the stage of life. Commit your best and in the process you will become your best. The central curriculum of life on Earth is a study in the art of being a human being. Remember to take your developmental steps a bit at a time based on your ability to expand without creating resistance.

- Purchase a Time Management System
- Shrink Story Boards and Mind Maps to fit system
- Purchase a Four-Color Pen
- Remember to Remember that the body suit was built to learn
- Create and sustain the Mental Climate for Optimal Learning
- Use Inclusive Sorting method
- Come from Possibility
- Be courageous; embrace life
- Observe life experience to determine development and input correction along the way
- Create and engage in answering your life questions through Sleep Programming and listening to life as it unfolds in people and experiences that are sent to you.
- Use Brain Shorthand and Power Notes
- Mind Maps for memory recall
- Use PFA for accelerated learning
- Use Whole Body Listening to grok Power Points
- Write your Vision Plan
- Use Self-Cultivation method
- Write Seed-States bimonthly
- Center daily and Visualize Seed-State
- Use Modeling and "act as if" frame wherever possible
- Find a Mentor for path of long-term mastery
- Use Sleep for problem solving
- Create and sustain healthy habits

Check off the things on this list that you have already made a part of your daily practice. Then choose one or two things that you want to add to your repertoire. Be satisfied to spend as much time as it takes to stabilize the activities or states that you have chosen. As they become habit and you know that they are fully integrated into your lifestyle, pick another item on which to focus.

As you utilize the learning states, the working tools and the daily centering you will begin to experience subtle shifts in both awareness and productivity. This marks the development of the *Learning to Learn* mind set. A few weeks after taking one of our business classes, a student named Tari reported back with outstanding results. She said that she had gone to a seminar with hundreds of people from different organizations. During the course of the day she found that she was "groking" the material on a whole new level and taking copious colorful notes a la *Learning to Learning* style. As time went on she noticed a few people staring at her, and when class was over one of them approached her requesting a copy of her fabulous, unusual notes. Fascinated by the technique, he asked if she'd be willing to share it with him. Naturally she was thrilled.

She went on to say that *Learning to Learn* had changed her life. Not only had she accelerated her learning time, but she was experiencing a felt-shift in her ability to listen, comprehend, and focus. It was as if the "ceiling" had been taken off and she was soaring in an open-ended sky.

CHARACTER OPPORTUNITIES

Enhanced productivity and effectiveness are the byproducts of *Learning to Learn,* but as Tari and many others have told us, that is not the total yield of the harvest. People are finding that the full harvest begins to show itself in the open territory of their lives. Not only is there a difference in their perspective regarding life and learning, but they also report a difference in the very way in which they encounter the daily personal and professional challenges that life delivers.

As we unlock the doorways of consciousness we begin to awaken to the unlimited performance potential available to us.

Mind generates Thought...Thoughts lead to Actions...Repeated Actions form Behavioral Patterns...Behavioral Patterns eventually become Habits...Habits etch deep to form Character...And, Character finally determines the Destiny of a Human Being.

Know that you are connected: A cell in the body of infinite life. This book is about learning to depend upon and expand that connectedness. It is no accident that it has found its way into your hands. Your readiness for the information has called it to you.

As we accept and expand our connectedness, we discover that life events that once looked like road blocks have become exercises in mastery. In a world where connectedness is experienced, obstacles are viewed as character opportunities in disguise.

Here is the place where I chance an encounter with my own development and can measure my distance toward my self-cultivation goal. Here, in this moment, is an opportunity for greater mastery.

Be ever alert to these character opportunities available in the daily events of your life. Unlike Hide and Seek, you won't find that you have to look in hidden places. Character opportunities are occurring everywhere all the time. They are happening when that car cuts in front of you on the freeway and nobody is there to observe your reaction but you. They are happening when deadlines are pressing in and tensions are rising at the office. They are happening when you are tired at the end of the day and the spouse or children need some extra attention.

Most of the time our lives are devoid of this alertness to our experience and as a result we have a track record full of missed opportunities. But an opportunity, even when caught after the fact, is still an opportunity. At the end of each day, review the events of that day looking for the places where you could have performed at a higher level. Use the moments of lesser mastery as an opportunity to rehearse for greater mastery. Center, be still, and re-run the event on your mental screen until you perform it perfectly.

FAST FORWARD TO THE FUTURE

Creative imagination forms the bridge between the world of dreams and the world of manifestation. To activate and sustain your personal training program, start with a blueprint of your personal best. Carefully choose the qualities you want to assimilate. Then develop a clear and consistent picture, for the high mind that guides and guards us needs an unwavering image in order to pour the energy of life into the mold.

Fast forward your film to the future and imagine that you are everything you always wanted to be. Visualize yourself unfettered and free, at the apex of development. As you view yourself, notice the specific qualities that you have chosen and fill in the vibrant details of perfection. Envision the supreme achievement: wisdom, compassion, empathy, creativity and the living of the life triumphant.

Before entering into the world of activity each day, take a moment to embrace this blueprint of transformation. Hold it before your mind's eye. Trace its features and experience the feelings of success and achievement. Make the vision so vivid that its energy permeates both your aura and the atmosphere around you, transforming your reality. As your life journey continues to unfold, you shall find yourself beginning to merge with the visionary blueprint that you've held.

In closing, let me leave you with a precious little gem, a true story that was shared with me by a friend who holds a black belt in Karate. This story has buoyed me up when I was down and rekindled the fires of inspiration when I needed it. May it do the same for you, and may your life be ever full as it unfolds in its magical miraculous way.

Once there was a great Karate Master whose ranking was of the tenth level black belt, of which there are only about 250 in all the world. His Dojo was known as the best throughout the land and he personally trained all the young black belts of the first level to be the finest and most noble trainers in the arena of Martial Arts. The black belts who graduated under his guiding hand were highly skilled and honorable men.

On the first Friday night of every month all the young black belts in training would gather in the main Dojo to perform individually before the master so that he might see their level of development and coach them on specific movements. The young black belts sat in a semicircle at the far end of the room facing the master. One by one they left the group to go before the master and individually perform their specific Kata - set of movements. After completion he would acknowledge their learning and growth.

On one such Friday evening, a young black belt came before him, bowed, took his position, and began his Kata. The master watched for a few moments as the young man performed, then he leaned forward with intense concentration, his hands grabbing the arms of his chair. Finally he leaped from his seat and with a stunning shout faced both the boy and the crowd of young men behind him.

"No! No! No!," he shouted. "You do not understand," he continued in very broken English, "If you practice just one of the moves for one minute every single day, then in six years you will be six years older, and you will have mastered that move." He paused for a moment, turning slowly to contact each member of the group, and then he continued with quiet brevity. "But if you do not practice just one minute a day, then in six years, you be six years older, but you be no master!"

A quiet hush fell over the Dojo, for the students knew the truth of the master's words, and each was made, in that instant, to look within their hearts to the depth of their personal commitment to mastery.

●●●

And the end becomes the beginning. Now that you have completed this book, go back and start over. The vision and aspirations represented here are lofty for every soul has a noble calling. As you read and re-read this manual for self-development, may your heart and spirit be lifted to greater heights. Remember, you are a cell in the great body of mankind, and as such, you have a very special contribution to make to our planet.

Begin your personal mastery today!

POWER POINTS

❀

As we consciously expand our Comfort Zone with
healthy habits, we free ourselves to focus on the
bigger picture of our lives.

❀

That which is unconscious runs our behavior.

❀

Create healthy habits, and healthy habits will carry
you when you need them.

❀

The central curriculum on Planet Earth is the study in
the art of being a human being. Life is our laboratory
for learning and growth in the human experience.

❀

As we unlock the doors of consciousness we awaken
to our unlimited performance potential.

❀

Know that you are a cell in the body of infinite life
and expand your connectedness with all.

❀

Rehearse, prepare, practice and perfect for we are
living but a short time upon the stage of life.

GLOSSARY
OF
TERMS

GLOSSARY

Body Suit: A term used to refer to the physical body that we wear on Planet Earth as distinct from the being who inhabits it. The human body suit was built to learn. The being resides in the body in order to live here and learn the lessons available in Earth's clasroom.

Blocks to Learning: Any unconscious beliefs, attitudes and perceptions that limit our ability to receive or retrieve information. The most common blocks to learning include *fear of failure, fear of success, low self-esteem, lack of self-confidence, an "I already got it" attitude, judgment, lack of willingness, and negative peer pressure.* The blocks to learning must be removed in order to realize our full performance potential.

Brain Shorthand: The recorded notations of quiet intimations that float into awareness bearing solutions to problems or delivering answers to questions that we may be working on. By taking brain shorthand, we are able to capture the whisperings of eternity, thus maximizing our performance potential and fulfilling our destiny.

Centering: The conscious inducement of deep relaxation that leads to mental stillness. It is a requisite for higher-order thinking for it enhances our ability to receive, retrieve, and integrate what we've learned. Centering, focusing, and meditation techniques will become central themes in future strategies for developing solutions to the challenges we are facing at every level in society. When we still the mind through daily centering, we begin to receive flashes of inspiration and insight from the great universal storehouse of wisdom.

Character Opportunities: Any seeming obstacles in our path that might deliver an opportunity to practice patience, service, silence, or any of the great attributes of a human being. Character opportunities show up everywhere: on the freeway when someone cuts in front of us, in line at the grocery store or bank, with our spouse or children when we have seemingly reached the limit of our energy or patience. Every character opportunity occurs at the edge of our Comfort Zone thus allowing us a chance to develop greater personal mastery over our emotions and our mind.

Classroom Planet Earth: In reference to the fact that Planet Earth is a classroom and that our life here is a learning journey, the aim of which is an experience in being a human being. The curriculum in Earth's classroom includes character development, kindness, compassion and wisdom.

Context and Content: Context and content are critical distinctions in the communication process. Context is like the container, content is what is placed in the container. The context that the communicator delivers will shape the way the content will be received by the listener; context sets up the listening. We empower the communication process when we create a powerful context at the beginning of our interaction. A truly powerful context raises the level of the content (i.e. the space suit story at the beginning of the book) and opens the door to a new domain of possibility.

Comfort Zone: The zone of comfortable behavior for any given individual. Everyone has a Comfort Zone and learning and growth pushes us to expand it. Each individual's Comfort Zone is made up of their planetary, cultural, and family imprinting as well as the habits that they have formed over time. To expand our Comfort Zone, we must be williing to change our thoughts, attitudes and beliefs, for these three shape our reality and direct our behavior.

Domain of possibility: The area or realm from which "miracles" occur. When we enter the domain of possibility, all universal energy is available to us for we contact the unified field from which all creation pours forth. The domain of possibility is without limitations, thus, we are free to create a future of our choosing.

Education: Education comes from the root word educere which means to draw out. True education is the drawing out of our latent and full performance potential. The end result of education is not intellect but the evolution of character which leads to wisdom.

GLOSSARY

Empowerment: To give someone the ability to act or perform in an effective way is to empower. To imbue with power or energy. Empowerment is a 21st century leadership principle.

Exclusive Sorting: The method of sorting incoming sensory information that separates the individual from the learning experience or the teacher. Exclusive sorting isolates the individual and disempowers the individual's learning process by closing off the domain of possibility that the environment may be offering at any given moment. Exclusive sorting immediately precludes the possibility of rapid change or growth by defending the status quo. Notice your inner dialogue; words such as *but, however* or *because* often reveal an exclusive sorting process. When you catch your inner dialogue precluding the possibility of change, turn it around.

Fight or Flight Response: The physical reflexive system for dealing with perceived environmental threats. The fight or flight response mobilizes our physical energies for external activity: to either fight the sensed threat or run from it. Neurochemicals are released in the brain, glucose floods the system, and blood is shunted from the brain to the muscles for muscular activity. The learning potential of an individual drops sharply during the fight or flight response.

Framing: There are two types of framing: how we frame our experience, and how we frame our conversations with others. In either case the frame is like a small context in that it shapes and colors the way we either hold our experience or ask the receiver in a conversation to hold the content that we are about to deliver. Framing is one of the most critical aspects of communication in that it establishes listening. Changing the color of a frame on a picture highlights the content of the picture. Changing the conversational frame highlights aspects of the conversation by directing the listener's focus. Many breakdowns occur in communication because people neglect giving careful attention to this initial stage in the communication cycle. For example, here's the difference framing can make when a parent wants his child to clean his or her room:

"Your room is always a mess, how come you don't ever clean it?"
"Your room is a mess, why don't you clean it!"

193

"Honey it's Saturday morning, let's clean up as quickly as possible so that we can have the rest of the weekend free to play and relax."
In the first two cases mom/dad has set the child up to be wrong and therefore created defensive listening. The natural result will be resistance. In the last frame, the parent empowered the child by focusing on the benefits of cleaning the room. If the vocal tone matched the frame, there is a good chance that the child would be receptive to the suggestion.

Function of the Mind: *The function of the mind is to merge with what it focuses on.* Herein lies the primary law of the physical body suit. This law of cause explains a myriad of effects in the physical universe. It explains why children, when they become adults, often develop the same habits that their parents had regardless of whether they liked the trait in their parent(s) or not. It also explains why we become what we love, for whether we are in love with something or resisting it, we are focusing our attention on it. Because the function of the mind is to merge, where we put our attention is where we get the result. On the other hand, by right use of this law all human beings can free themselves from the limiting chains of the past. Love what is good and we become good; focus on men and women who are models of excellence and we raise our level of excellence.

Ganus: A Spanish word that covers a myriad of emotions from willingness to fervor, from enthusiasm to zeal. To have the ganus is to have the desire, passion, spirit, zest, yearning, and aspiration for something. Ganus is the fuel that fires the engine for learning.

Groking: Groking occurs naturally when we practice whole body listening. To grok something is to grasp it: to get the marrow, the inner meaning, the crux, or the gist of it. To get the essence of a communication or sharing such that we are able to recreate it in our own language. By practicing groking, we can all become contributors to the planetary evolution.Groking enables us to learn quickly and to share what we have learned with others.

Inclusive Sorting: The method of sorting incoming sensory information that merges the individual with the learning experience and the teacher. The attitude of a person who sorts information inclusively is, "If he can do it, I can do it too!" Inclusive sorting liberates our performance potential by enabling us to hold everyone who is more developed then we are in any given area as a model of possibility rather than a reason for inadequacy. Inclusive sorting also helps us view all learning experiences as character opportunities in disguise. An exclusive sorting mechanism might be, "Why is this happening to me?" While an inclusive sorting mechanism would be, "This is happening to me to develop attributes such as patience, stillness, humility, commitment, discipline, etc."

Infinite Mind: The term infinite mind is used here in reference to the infinite mind of a human being. Intelligence is elastic and is not localized in the brain. It is located throughout the body at the cellular level and extends in an inter-connective web with the grand intelligence of the universe, which we refer to as Universal Mind purely for purposes of clarification. In truth, Infinite mind and Universal Mind overlap and are as intricately interwoven as a spider web. Neither can exist without the other; we are part and parcel of an interdependent universe.

Inner Work: The inner work is anything and everything that we do on the inner level that enhances the transformation of consciousness and thus transforms our outer behavior or experience. This includes centering, changing your self-talk, reframing your experience and visualization. It is the inner work that brings peace and tranquility to the restless mind; as we become conduits rather than controllers life begins to work through us and our contribution to our community naturally expands.

Law of the Unconscious: *That which is unconscious runs our behavior.* This refers to all the unconscious patterns that have been either imprinted or programmed into the subconscious mind. These unconscious patterns become the drivers of behavior.

Life Works: The full phrase is "life works, get out of the way and let it!" This phrase refers to life's ever-expansive, ever growth oriented all pervading way! If we will just become conduits, life will flow through us. Life always succeeds, so let it happen!

Memory Moment: A memory moment is created as sensory information crosses the threshold of our awareness and an intuitive emotional response to it is recorded. As the body receives these sensory, intuitive, emotional memory moment packets, it translates them into electrochemical impulses and stores them throughout the brain and body. In order to retrieve those images we need only think of part of the original image or sensation (an aspect of the sight, sound, smell, or emotion) and the entire image or thought can be easily retrieved. Because the natural language of the brain is sensory-based, the more senses we involve in the learning process the easier memory retrieval becomes.

Mind Map: A mind map is a learning enhancement tool that aids memory retrieval. Formed like a tree, the mind map's trunk contains the main subject at its center. The branches are made up of the main topics, and the twigs contain the ideas pertaining to those main topics. While excellent for note taking, information gathering, or record keeping with clients or co-workers, mind maps prove most valuable when it comes to idea generation and memory access. Every mind map begins with the question, "What do I know about...." The mind-mapping process releases quantities of information into conscious awareness by opening the doorway to the storehouse of the subconscious. A key advantage of using the mind map is that we can quickly and precisely locate blind spots on any given subject.

Modeling: Modeling is observing and taking on the attributes of a great human being. Modeling is a master key to success because it utilizes the three mental keys of attention, imagination and focus. Modeling is the fast track to mastery because it is the ability to instantly imagine or "put on" the attributes of another human being. Learning is accelerated when we assimilate the lessons of others. What we model is what we become!

New Paradigm: A new model for the 21st century that focuses on teamwork, adaptability, flexibility, creativity, innovation, and the human side of enterprise in both our professional and personal lives.

Performance Potential: The limitless latent capacity of all human beings to perform exquisitely and effectively. As human beings our performance potential needs to be tapped so that we can meet the challenges of the 21st century in new and innovative ways.

Power Notes: A simple method of taking notes that utilizes the natural processing procedure of the brain. This system makes it easy to access an entire body of knowledge from a small amount of written data. This note-taking system is based on the fact that the brain records all incoming sensory information in single-unit memory moments. The key to using Power Notes is to grasp the essence of meaning, translate it into our own language and record the most powerful points portrayed in colorful, magical, symbolic ways.

PFA - Present Field Awareness: PFA integrates inner and outer awareness. By using PFA we expand our awareness beyond our body suits to include the field of information that surrounds us. Through PFA we induce a state of heightened acuity and receptivity to the full field or environment. Thus, learning is enhanced. Done in conjunction with daily centering, PFA expands awareness, and helps induce the alpha brain wave state. As we experience ourselves as a field of awareness and not a form with boundaries, the inner world and the outer world begin to merge and true intuitive knowing occurs.

Process + Product =Outcome: Process is the "how" of learning; it is the way we go about learning. Product is the "what" of learning; it is the material or curriculum with which we are working. The outcome is the end result and it includes both the skills and character abilities developed in the process, as well as the material or the product learned.

RAS: The Reticular Activating System is a bundle of nerve fibers about the size of the tip of your small finger located at the base of the brain stem. It's purpose is to filter incoming sensory information to avoid sensory overload. The RAS has two functions: (1) it controls the level of volume on incoming information; and (2) it directs our attention by tuning in to what we deem important and tuning out what we are not interested in at the moment. It is the RAS that allows us to focus our attention on a specific task at hand while tuning out sights and sounds extraneous to our immediate purpose.

Relaxation Response: A phrase coined by Herbert Benson, the relaxation response can be learned to relieve stress and anxiety and ameliorate constant low-grade arousal in our bodies. When relaxed, the brain's electrical activity drops and oxygen going to the brain increases, thus, increasing the body's natural ability to learn and retain information.

Remember to Remember: A term that is always used in reference to a wake-up call of some kind. Remember to Remember who you are: A wake-up call to remember that you are a being living in a body. Remember to Remember why you're here: A wake-up call to remember that you are here to contribute to life on Earth in some small way.

R=D+S: The amount of resistance is equal to the distance that we travel out of our Comfort Zone plus the speed with which the move is executed. In other words, the amount of resistance that we create to change will be equivalent to how far and how fast we leave our C-Zone, regardless of whether or not the change is good for us.

Seed-States: Seed-states are sensory-rich blueprints for change used in the self-cultivation process. They center around the characteristics that we eventually want to mold into our character.

Self-Cultivation: Self-cultivation is a lifelong learning model for behavioral change based on the metaphor of the seed in the soil. Self-cultivation is mental gardening; the planting and nurturing of healthy seed thoughts. It is the means by which we can achieve all of our behavioral and skill development goals. Self-cultivation leads to refinement of character, and ultimately, to the fulfillment of our destiny.

Story Boards: Originally used by Walt Disney, story boards record one frame or one moment of our experience at a time. As we record our power notes on story boards, we later find ourselves able to access an entire body of knowledge from a small amount of written data.

Turn Failure Into Feedback: Every small failure is an "after-the-fact" character opportunity in disguise. By reviewing, analyzing and correcting all of our mistakes, these small failures become feedback and thus opportunities for learning and growth. By turning all of our mistakes into opportunities for learning and growth, we begin to maximize our performance potential. Mistakes are part and parcel of the discovery process; the "wrong" way is the avenue through which the "right" way is discovered.

Vision Plan: Vision Planning creates the context for life change and gently directs the course of both personal and professional transformation. Vision Planning maintains the structural integrity of the body suit's natural learning ability. A vision plan has the power to transform routine daily activities into magic by fueling the fire of our personal Ganus. As we clarify our vision we move one step closer to the goal of becoming self-inspired, self-actualized humans.

What Does It Mean To Be A Human Being?: The fundamental question that should be at the heart of every course curriculum with its antecedent question...Why Am I Here?

Whole Body Listening: This method of listening turns hearing into a whole body experience and heightens both receptivity and mental acuity. Whole body listening expands perception and allows intuitive whisperings and sensations to be experienced. Whole body listening enhances communication personally and professionally.

Universal Mind: The term universal mind is used in reference to the infinite intelligence of the universe which is available to us at all times. All we have to do to "tune in" to universal mind. We must stop our minds by fully focusing our awareness on a still point within. To get answers to questions or solutions to problems, all we have to do is clarify the question or problem, then release it and silence our mind. When we are completely still our inner receptivity becomes a metaphorical lightning rod attracting the electrically energized answer. If you do not get an immediate answer (within 20 minutes or so) go about your daily business maintaining this inner receptivity. Usually the answer will arrive within a day or two. Universal mind's delivery system is often extremely creative for it transcends physical law and thus can use the physical universe as its personal speedy delivery system.

APPENDIX

APPENDIX

The Brain's Electrical Activity (Chapter 5)

In order to understand these fluctuations and the resultant experience that these fluctuations reflect, we have included a brief description of the differences in the four brain wave measurements.

BETA 14-30 CPS*
External awareness
External attention and activity
Ordinary states of consciousness

ALPHA 7-14 CPS
Beginning of relaxation response
Heightened creativity
Hemispheric synchronization begins in lower ranges

THETA 3-7 CPS
Hemispheric synchronization
Whole brain sensory integration high
Unified field experience - "peak experience" feeling
Potential for optimal learning extremely high
Receptivity to inner visioning extremely high
Vivid memory recall/high intuitive idea generation
Heightened state for processing and storage of information

DELTA 1-3 CPS
Deep sleep state

*CPS means cycles per second as measured on an EEG.

As we can see, the obvious goal for rapid learning is the theta brain wave state. Not only do we achieve hemispheric synchronization in this range, but there is also a heightening of mental acuity, intuitive awareness, and creativity, as well as vivid memory recall. Further studies reveal that this relaxed state leads to superior performance in all areas. In general, the theta range of activity is the range that produces enhanced abilities in both young and old alike.

APPENDIX

OTHER COMPLETED EXAMPLES OF SEED-STATES (Chpts. 14,15)

Initiative (professional)

I actively initiate and execute projects based on proper planning and timely scheduling. I can see myself at my desk in the planning stage, organizing my thoughts on paper. Learning to Learn music is playing softly in the background as I begin scheduling and dating the targets on my calendar. The plan is so clear that I am ready to move on it immediately and I hear myself calling my secretary into the office to discuss the initial stages with me. She is thrilled at the plan and says that she will be easily able to help me achieve it. It feels great to be in control of my time and energies.

Procrastination (getting rid of it!)

I do everything that needs to be done as it needs doing. I enjoy this feeling of timeliness and order and so do the people around me. I can see my in-basket at the end of the day and it is empty. I see myself checking off completions on my project deadlines and I hear my co-workers acknowledging me for a timely job well done. It feels great to be so relaxed and focused as I move confidently forward in the step by step achievement of my long-range goals.

Communication (personal)

I easily communicate my deepest fears and feelings with my spouse. I can see us sitting by the fireplace in the early evening sharing our thoughts about life and living. As I share my need to be supported in the next stage of my growth, I can feel that he has his needs too. We share our goals and the barriers that we are facing, and as we do, the soft glow of color in the room seems to fill our hearts too. It feels great to be able to communicate fully with my partner and to know that our support will always be there for each other.

Communication (on a specific project)

I communicate effectively and easily during our staff meetings. I can see myself standing in front of the group. My demeanor is poised, relaxed and confident as I adjust the overhead chart on the screen. I notice that my steering committee is responding warmly to my new proposal for training in the coming year. There is a growing excitement in the air as I continue talking about the possibilities that the future holds for all of us. Finally we take a vote and I see every hand in the room agreeing to go with my plan. The unanimous agreement for the plan is astounding!

BAROQUE PLUS

Sixteenth- to eighteenth-century composers Bach, Vivaldi, Corelli, Handel and Telemann produced music referred to as Baroque. Researchers believe Baroque music affects us by aligning, synchronizing both mind and body to more harmonious patterns. Suggested music and music sources:

Bach, J.S.
* *Arioso*
Corelli, A.
* *Largo from Concerti Grossi No. 3*
Handel, G.F.
* Largo from Concerto No. 3 in D (brass) from *Music for the Royal Fireworks*
Vivaldi, A.
* Largo from "Winter" from *The Four Seasons*
  Lola Bobesco, violin, The Heidelberg Chamber Orchestra, Peerless Records.

Other sources of music found conducive to enhanced learning:
* *Lazaris & The Dolphins*
* *Lazaris Remembers Lemuria*
* *Journey with Lazaris*
* *Prelude to Lazaris*

•••

Pachelbel
Invincible Recordings
P.O. 13054 Phoenix, Arizona 85002
Path of Joy by Daniel Kobialka
Li-Sem Enterprises
1775 Old Country Road #9 Belmont, California 94002
Concept Synergy
P.O. Box 159 M Fairfax, California 94930
Élan Enterprises
47-430 Hui Nene St. Kaneohe, Hawaii 96744

EYE EXERCISES

Eye exercises to enhance sensory awareness and accelerate learning:

It has been said that the eyes are the windows to the soul and in recent times we have found them to be the doorways to consciousness. The eyes move in a consistent manner when we are accessing information from memory or creatively planning something for the future.

Therefore, we can utilize eye exercises to enhance and stimulate both memory and creativity. The following seven simple stimulation points, done as a daily exercise, will open vast amouonts of awareness over time. hold each position for 15-20 seconds before moving to the next one.

- **Visual recall** or memory: eyes up and to the left.
- **Auditory recall or memory:** eyes down and to the left and eyes horizontally left.
- **Visual creativity:** eyes up and to the right.
- **Kinesthetic memory (feelings or emotions):** eyes down and to the right.
- **Auditory creativity:** eyes horizontally to the right.
- **Visual, auditory and kinesthetic** merged and integrated, eyes gazing past nose and defocused.
- **Intuition:** eyes focued on a spot between eyebrows. This is known as the Third Eye Center in Eastern tradition and is the seat of intuition or direct knowing.

Practicing these seven positions will only take about 2-3 minutes daily. However, the benefits for such stimulation are vast. Attention is energy and when we put our attention on these memory and creativity centers we stimulate their awakenings.

SOURCES

Benson, Herbert and Miriam Klipper. *The Relaxation Response*. New York: Avon Books, 1984.

Campbell, Joseph. *The World of Joseph Campbell: Joseph Campbell on His Life and Work*. San Francisco: Harper and Row Publishing Co., 1990.

Capra, Fritjof. *The Tao of Physics*. Boston: Shambhla Publications, 1991.

Erikson, Erik H. *Childhood and Society*. New York: Norton Publishing Co., 1964.

Gendlin, Eugene. *Focusing*. New York: Bantam Books, 1982.

Heinlin, Robert. *Stranger in a Strange Land*. New York: Ace Books; Berkley Publishing Co., 1991.

Hutchison, Michael. *MEGABRAIN*. New York: Ballantine Books; Random House, Inc., 1986.

Maltz, Maxwell. *Psycho-Cybernetics*. Inglewood Cliffs: Prentice Hall, Inc., 1960.

Smigel, Lloyd Merrit. *Handle With Care: A Guide to Managing U.S. Employees in the 1990s*. Oceanside: Care Management, 1989.

POWER NOTES

POWER NOTES

POWER NOTES

ÉLAN ENTERPRISES

D. Trinidad Hunt • Lynne M. Truair

Our goal at Élan Enterprises is to produce and disseminate materials in the spirit of true humanity. *Learning to Learn - Maximizing Your Performance Potential*, and its companion audiocassette series, offer specific learning skills designed for 21st century effectiveness.

These skills are also the basis for our highly successful corporate training programs. With more than 35 organizational programs, we tailor training to suit your specific goals and needs.

The Academy Élan, discussed throughout this book, is a training ground for individuals seeking mastery, and an outstanding personal and professional enhancement program for community and business leaders, offered in Hawaii, Wisconsin, and Canada.

- ## Training for the 21st Century
  More than 35 corporate training programs available:
    - Change Management
    - Leadership
    - Learning Skills
    - Service
    - Teamwork
    - Self-Esteem
    - Communication

- ## World Youth Network International
  Co-founded in 1996, WYN International's mission is to provide today's youth with life skills that will help them succeed in the 21st century. Youth retreats, parent & teacher training.

- ## Keynote Speaking

• The Academy Élan

A learning laboratory which offers an integrated course curriculum of work, play and humor to release the latent potential in each individual.

A series of 3 individual weekend retreats are focusing on *The Power of Personal Purpose, The Power of Personal Myth, and Discovering Your Energy Effect.*

• Product Line

Educational and inspirational books and audiocassette tapes by D. Trinidad Hunt. The following materials are available:

Learning to Learn - Maximizing Your Performance Potential
Available in paperback, on audiocassettes, and supplemental music on audiocassettes for centering and learning enhancement.

Remember to Remember Who You Are
Pocket-sized book of inspirational verses and poems

The Operator's Manual for Planet Earth -
An Adventure for the Soul
A modern metaphor to live by,
a new mythology for a new generation

For more information regarding
Élan Enterprises' corporate training programs,
seminars, to order products, or to be on
our mailing list, call or write today:

47-430 Hui Nene St.
Kaneohe, Hawaii 96744
(800) 707-ELAN, Fax (808) 239-2482
Email: elantrin@aol.com
Website: http://speakers.com/trin.html

ORDER FORM

PLEASE SEND ME THE FOLLOWING BY
D. TRINIDAD HUNT

#	TITLE	PRICE	TOTAL
	BOOKS		
	Learning to Learn: *-Maximizing Your Performance Potential-*	$10.95	
	Remember to Remember Who You Are	$ 5.95	
	The Operator's Manual for Planet Earth *-An Adventure for the Soul-*	$19.95	
	AUDIO CASSETTES		
	Learning to Learn Audio Supplement Two cassettes offering exercises in: Centering, Present Field Awareness & Original Music to Enhance Learning	$12.95	
	Learning to Learn BOOK on TAPE	$49.95	

Subtotal _____

Shipping and Handling (add 20% of subtotal) _____

Hawaii Residents add 4.167 % Tax _____

TOTAL $ _____

SHIP TO:

_____

NAME

_____

ADDRESS

_____

CITY/STATE/ZIPCODE   PHONE NUMBER

Card # _____ Exp. Date _____

Check, Money Order, Visa, MasterCard Accepted
For orders outside of the U.S., please call for prices
Elan Enterprises Press
47-430 Hui Nene St. Kaneohe, Hawaii 96744
ph. (800) 707-ELAN fax (808) 239-2482